S0-BZK-106

Goose berry Patch®

Keep it Simple.   Make it Special.

Comfort Food
Lightened Up

Dedication

For every cook that wants to live healthier by making classic comfort food recipes that are lightened up and delicious!

Appreciation

Thanks to everyone who shared their very favorite, lightened-up comfort food recipes with us!

Gooseberry Patch
An imprint of Globe Pequot
246 Goose Lane • Guilford, CT 06437

www.gooseberrypatch.com
1·800·854·6673

Copyright 2016, Gooseberry Patch 978-1-62093-226-1
First Printing, 2016

Table of Contents

Recipe Notes & Nutrition Facts

Comfort food can be light and healthy as well as delicious. The recipes in this book were chosen or developed to be lighter and healthier than some of the recipes you may have used in the past. This means they may contain fewer calories, less fat, less salt, less sugar or more fiber. At the bottom of each recipe, you will see that each recipe has been analyzed to determine the nutritional content of the recipe. To help you understand what the values mean in these nutritional analyses, we recommend that you compare them to the FDA's recommended values.

CALCULATING THE NUTRITIONAL ANALYSIS WHEN USING THE FOLLOWING:

▶ **Salt and pepper to taste:** When the recipe indicates this, salt and pepper were not included in the nutritional analysis.

▶ **For frostings:** When testing recipes, we based the nutritional analysis on what was actually used or shown in the photo.

▶ **For dressings:** When the recipe calls for dressing, the entire dressing recipe was assumed to be used and all is included in the nutritional analysis.

▶ **For sauces:** When testing the recipes, we based the nutritional analysis on the amount of sauce that was actually used per serving, not including extra leftover sauce.

The following are the FDA's daily recommendations for an adult eating a 2000 calorie per day diet. You can refer to these numbers as you are looking at the nutritional values of the recipes in this book. Of course if you are a larger or active person, you probably have higher nutritional needs, and if you are a smaller or sedentary person, you probably have lower nutritional needs. In addition, children, and pregnant and lactating women have unique nutritional needs.

FDA DAILY RECOMMENDATIONS FOR THE AVERAGE AMERICAN ADULT:

Total Calories:	2000 calories
Total Fat:	65g
Saturated Fat:	20g
Cholesterol:	300mg
Sodium:	2400mg
Carbohydrates:	300g
Fiber:	25g
Protein:	50g

Note: Ingredients in a product can vary slightly according to brands and natural differences in the ingredients. The nutritional analyses were based on typical brands and ingredients of products available at the time of printing.

Under each recipe we have given a yield amount as well as a serving amount. The nutritional analysis is based on the serving amount. That is, the yield may be 24 cookies but it serves 12. That means that each person would be served 2 cookies.

U.S. to Metric Recipe Equivalents

Volume Measurements

1/4 teaspoon	1 mL
1/2 teaspoon	2 mL
1 teaspoon	5 mL
1 tablespoon = 3 teaspoons	15 mL
2 tablespoons = 1 fluid ounce	30 mL
1/4 cup	60 mL
1/3 cup	75 mL
1/2 cup = 4 fluid ounces	125 mL
1 cup = 8 fluid ounces	250 mL
2 cups = 1 pint = 16 fluid ounces	500 mL
4 cups = 1 quart	1 L

Weights

1 ounce	30 g
4 ounces	120 g
8 ounces	225 g
16 ounces = 1 pound	450 g

Oven Temperatures

300° F	150° C
325° F	160° C
350° F	180° C
375° F	190° C
400° F	200° C
450° F	230° C

Baking Pan Sizes

Square

8x8x2 inches	2 L = 20x20x5 cm
9x9x2 inches	2.5 L = 23x23x5 cm

Rectangular

13x9x2 inches	3.5 L = 33x23x5 cm

Loaf

9x5x3 inches	2 L = 23x13x7 cm

Round

8x1-1/2 inches	1.2 L = 20x4 cm
9x1-1/2 inches	1.5 L = 23x4 cm

Recipe Abbreviations

t. = teaspoon	ltr. = liter
T. = tablespoon	oz. = ounce
c. = cup	lb. = pound
pt. = pint	doz. = dozen
qt. = quart	pkg. = package
gal. = gallon	env. = envelope

Kitchen Measurements

A pinch = 1/8 tablespoon	1 fluid ounce = 2 tablespoons
3 teaspoons = 1 tablespoon	4 fluid ounces = 1/2 cup
2 tablespoons = 1/8 cup	8 fluid ounces = 1 cup
4 tablespoons = 1/4 cup	16 fluid ounces = 1 pint
8 tablespoons = 1/2 cup	32 fluid ounces = 1 quart
16 tablespoons = 1 cup	16 ounces net weight = 1 pound
2 cups = 1 pint	
4 cups = 1 quart	
4 quarts = 1 gallon	

Classic Starters & Snacks

(tasty light bites)

Lighten up the party with a sampling of these classic starters and snacks that everyone will enjoy! Share some Simple Tomato Bruschetta on whole-grain toast, serve Tangy Meatballs made with heart-healthy oatmeal and enjoy Chili Sweet Potato Fries baked to perfect crispiness! Whether you are preparing an appetizer for that special party or just a snack to tide you over to the next meal, make it a healthy version of those favorite comfort foods you love so much. Good for you!

Prosciutto-Wrapped Asparagus

Serves 6.

1 bunch asparagus, about 12 pieces, trimmed
1 T. olive oil
1 t. kosher salt
1 t. pepper
3-oz. pkg. sliced prosciutto, cut into strips with
   fat removed
Optional: lemon slices

Toss asparagus with oil, salt and pepper. Arrange in a single layer on an ungreased rimmed baking sheet. Bake at 400 degrees for 5 minutes. Allow to cool slightly.

Prosciutto-Wrapped Asparagus

Wrap each asparagus spear with a strip of prosciutto. Return to oven and bake for 4 more minutes or until asparagus is crisp-tender and prosciutto is slightly browned. Serve warm or at room temperature, garnished with lemon slices if desired.

Nutrition Per Serving: *50 calories, 3g total fat, 1g sat fat, 13mg cholesterol, 610mg sodium, 1g carbohydrate, 1g fiber, 5g protein*

Tangy Meatballs

Makes 4 dozen. Serves 24.

2 lbs. lean ground beef
2 eggs, beaten
1/2 t. salt
3/4 c. quick-cooking oats, uncooked
1-1/3 c. chili sauce, divided
1/4 c. grape jelly
Optional: dried parsley

Combine ground beef, eggs, salt, oats and 1/3 cup chili sauce. Shape into one-inch balls; place in an ungreased shallow baking pan. Bake at 400 degrees for 15 to 17 minutes; drain. Combine grape jelly and remaining chili sauce in a large saucepan; cover and cook over medium heat, stirring occasionally until mixture is well blended. Add meatballs and continue cooking until heated through. Sprinkle with parsley, if desired.

Nutrition Per Serving: *126 calories, 7g total fat, 1g sat fat, 46mg cholesterol, 284mg sodium, 8g carbohydrate, 1g fiber, 8g protein*

Tangy Meatballs

Salmon Party Log

Salmon Party Log
Makes about 3 cups. Serves 24.

16-oz. can salmon, drained and flaked
8-oz. pkg. light cream cheese, softened
1 T. lemon juice
1 t. prepared horseradish
2 t. onion, grated
1/4 t. salt
1/4 t. low-sodium Worcestershire sauce
1/2 c. chopped pecans
3 T. fresh parsley, chopped
whole-grain crackers

Place all ingredients except pecans, parsley and crackers in a medium bowl. Mix thoroughly; shape into a log. Place pecans and parsley on wax paper; roll log in mixture until coated. Cover and chill at least 2 hours. Serve with crackers.

Nutrition Per Serving: 65 calories, 5g total fat, 1g sat fat, 18mg cholesterol, 148mg sodium, 1g carbohydrate, 0g fiber, 5g protein

Veggie Mini Pizzas
Serves 6.

6 pita rounds or flatbreads
1-1/2 c. pizza or pasta sauce
1 c. baby spinach
1 c. shredded low-fat mozzarella cheese
2 plum tomatoes, sliced

Place pita rounds on an ungreased baking sheet. Spread each with 1/4 cup sauce; top with spinach, cheese and tomato. Bake at 350 degrees for 15 to 20 minutes, or until cheese is bubbly.

Nutrition Per Serving: 158 calories, 4g total fat, 2g sat fat, 10mg cholesterol, 610mg sodium, 22g carbohydrate, 2g fiber, 7g protein

Quick tip
Let the kids lend a hand in the kitchen! Preschoolers can wash veggies, fold napkins and set the table. Older children can measure, stir and help with meal planning.

Veggie Mini Pizzas

Classic Starters & Snacks

Fresh Fruit Kabobs & Poppy Seed Dip

Fresh Fruit Kabobs & Poppy Seed Dip

Serves 10.

6 c. fresh fruit like strawberries, kiwi, pineapple, honeydew and cantaloupe, peeled and cut into bite-size cubes or slices
10 wooden skewers

Arrange fruit pieces alternately on skewers. Serve dip alongside fruit kabobs.

Nutrition Per Serving: 37 calories, 0g total fat, 0g sat fat, 0mg cholesterol, 12mg sodium, 9g carbohydrate, 1g fiber, 1g protein

Poppy Seed Dip

Serves 10.

1 c. low-fat vanilla yogurt
2 T. honey
4 t. lime juice
1 t. vanilla extract
1 t. poppy seed

Stir together ingredients in a small bowl. Keep chilled.

Nutrition Per Serving: 35 calories, 0g total fat, 0g sat fat, 2mg cholesterol, 16mg sodium, 7g carbohydrate, 0g fiber, 1g protein

Peggy's Granola

Makes about 14 cups. Serves 14.

4 c. quick-cooking oats, uncooked
2 c. crispy rice cereal
2 c. sliced almonds
2 T. cinnamon
1 c. brown sugar, packed
1/3 c. butter
1/2 c. honey
2 c. raisins or chopped dried fruit

Toss oats, cereal, almonds and cinnamon together in a large bowl; set aside. Combine brown sugar, butter and honey in a heavy saucepan over medium-high heat. Boil, stirring occasionally, until butter is melted and brown sugar is dissolved. Pour over oat mixture; stir to coat. Spread evenly on an aluminum foil-lined baking sheet. Bake at 350 degrees for 10 minutes; stir well. Bake for an additional 10 minutes. Remove from oven and cool 5 minutes; transfer to a large bowl. Stir in raisins or fruit and cool completely. Store in airtight containers.

Nutrition Per Serving: 417 calories, 17g total fat, 4g sat fat, 11mg cholesterol, 40mg sodium, 63g carbohydrate, 6g fiber, 8g protein

Honey Fruit Yogurt Dip

Party Nibblers
Makes about 6 cups. Serves 6.

1 c. cashews
1 c. peanuts
1 c. bite-size cheese crackers
1 c. bite-size shredded wheat cereal squares
1 c. bite-size shredded rice cereal squares
1 c. mini pretzels
2 T. grated Parmesan cheese
1/4 c. butter, melted
1 t. low-sodium Worcestershire sauce
1/2 t. celery salt
1/2 t. garlic powder

Combine nuts, crackers, cereals and pretzels in a large bowl; mix well and set aside. Whisk remaining ingredients together in a small bowl; pour over mix, tossing to coat. Spread in an ungreased 15"x10" jelly-roll pan; bake at 350 degrees for 15 to 20 minutes, stirring often. Cool completely; store in an airtight container.

Nutrition Per Serving: 416 calories, 28g total fat, 8g sat fat, 21mg cholesterol, 594mg sodium, 34g carbohydrate, 2g fiber, 12g protein

Honey Fruit Yogurt Dip
Makes about 1-1/2 cups. Serves 6.

1-1/3 c. non-fat plain Greek yogurt
2 t. honey
1/4 t. orange zest
1 T. orange juice
1/8 t. vanilla extract

Stir together all ingredients in a serving bowl. Cover and chill.

Nutrition Per Serving: 47 calories, 0g total fat, 0g sat fat, 4mg cholesterol, 31mg sodium, 5g carbohydrate, 0g fiber, 7g protein

Quick tip
Here's an easy way to core apples, pears and peaches. Slice fruit in half, then use a melon baller to scoop out the core.

Artichoke Frittata Squares

Artichoke Frittata Squares

Serves 12.

2 6-oz. jars marinated artichokes, drained and
  2 T. marinade reserved
4 eggs, beaten
1 c. low-fat ricotta cheese
1 onion, chopped
3/8 t. fresh rosemary
3/8 t. fresh thyme
3/8 t. fresh basil
1/8 t. dried marjoram

Finely chop artichokes; place in a bowl. Add reserved marinade and remaining ingredients; mix well. Spread mixture into a greased 8"x8" baking pan. Bake at 350 degrees for 30 minutes, or until set and golden. Cut into small rectangles; serve warm.

Nutrition Per Serving: 55 calories, 3g total fat, 1g sat fat, 77mg cholesterol, 64mg sodium, 2g carbohydrate, 0g fiber, 4g protein

Chinese Spareribs

Chinese Spareribs

Serves 15.

6 lbs. lean pork spareribs, sliced into serving-size
  portions
1/4 c. hoisin sauce
1/4 c. water
3 T. dry sherry
2 T. honey
1 T. low-sodium soy sauce
2 cloves garlic, minced

Place ribs in a very large plastic zipping bag. Mix remaining ingredients in a small bowl; pour over ribs. Seal bag; turn gently to coat ribs with marinade. Refrigerate for 6 hours to overnight, turning bag several times. Drain; reserve and refrigerate marinade. Place ribs in a lightly greased shallow roasting pan. Cover with aluminum foil. Bake at 350 degrees for 1-1/2 hours. Uncover; brush reserved marinade over ribs, discarding any remaining marinade. Bake, uncovered, an additional 30 minutes, or until tender.

Nutrition Per Serving: 380 calories, 30g total fat, 11g sat fat, 99mg cholesterol, 165mg sodium, 3g carbohydrate, 0g fiber, 22g protein

Classic Starters & Snacks

Crabmeat-Stuffed Eggs
Serves 24.

1 doz. eggs, hard-boiled, peeled and halved
1 c. crabmeat, flaked
1 c. celery, finely chopped
2 T. green pepper, finely chopped
1/8 c. plain yogurt
1 T. light mayonnaise
Garnish: thin green pepper slices

Scoop egg yolks into a bowl and mash with fork. Place egg whites on a serving dish and set aside. Combine mashed yolks and remaining ingredients except garnish; blend well. Spoon mixture into egg whites. Chill until serving time. Garnish, if desired.

Nutrition Per Serving: 80 calories, 5g total fat, 2g sat fat, 225mg cholesterol, 144mg sodium, 2g carbohydrate, 0g fiber, 8g protein

Gingered Salmon Skewers
Serves 12.

1 lb. boneless, skinless salmon fillet
12 wooden skewers, soaked in water
1/4 c. low-sodium soy sauce
1/4 c. honey
1 T. rice wine vinegar or cider vinegar
1 t. fresh ginger, peeled and minced
1 clove garlic, minced
1/8 t. pepper
lemon wedges

Slice salmon lengthwise into 12 narrow strips. Thread each strip onto a skewer; place skewers in a shallow dish. Whisk together soy sauce, honey, vinegar and spices. Pour over skewers, turning to coat. Let stand at room temperature for 30 minutes. Drain marinade into a small saucepan; simmer over medium-low heat for several minutes. Grill skewers over medium-high heat on a lightly-oiled grill, brushing often with marinade, for 4 minutes on each side. Squeeze lemon wedges over salmon; serve warm.

Nutrition Per Serving: 104 calories, 4g total fat, 1g sat fat, 33mg cholesterol, 188mg sodium, 6g carbohydrate, 0g fiber, 11g protein

Bruschetta with Cranberry Relish
Serves 16.

1 large whole-grain baguette loaf, sliced 1/4-inch thick
1 to 2 T. olive oil
1 t. orange zest
1 t. lemon zest
1/2 c. chopped pecans
1/2 c. crumbled low-fat blue cheese

Brush baguette slices lightly with oil. Arrange on a broiler pan; toast lightly under broiler. Turn slices over; spread with Cranberry Relish. Sprinkle with zests, pecans and blue cheese. Place under broiler just until cheese begins to melt.

Cranberry Relish:

16-oz. can whole-berry cranberry sauce
6-oz. pkg. sweetened dried cranberries
1/2 c. sugar
1 t. rum extract
1 c. chopped pecans

Stir all ingredients together.

Nutrition Per Serving: 225 calories, 9g total fat, 1g sat fat, 3mg cholesterol, 146mg sodium, 34g carbohydrate, 3g fiber, 5g protein

Bruschetta with Cranberry Relish

Homemade Guacamole

Homemade Guacamole

Makes about 2 cups. Serves 6.

3 avocados, pitted, peeled and mashed
1/2 c. tomato, chopped
1/4 c. onion, chopped
2 t. garlic, minced
1 T. fresh cilantro, chopped
1/2 t. salt
1 t. pepper
1 t. cayenne pepper
1 t. chili powder
1/2 t. hot pepper sauce
tortilla chips

Combine ingredients except tortilla chips in order listed.
Mix well; chill. Serve with tortilla chips.

Nutrition Per Serving: 246 calories, 24g total fat, 0g sat fat,
0mg cholesterol, 211mg sodium, 7g carbohydrate, 4g fiber,
2g protein

Seeded Tortilla Crisps

Pita Chips

Serves 8.

4 6-inch whole-wheat pita rounds, split
6 t. olive oil
2 cloves garlic, pressed

Cut each split pita round in half; cut each half into
4 triangles. In a small bowl, combine olive oil and garlic
in a small bowl; brush over triangles. Arrange triangles
in a single layer on an ungreased baking sheet. Bake at
350 degrees for 8 to 10 minutes, until crisp and golden.

Nutrition Per Serving: 100 calories, 4g total fat, 0g sat fat,
0mg cholesterol, 160mg sodium, 15g carbohydrate, 2g fiber,
1g protein

Seeded Tortilla Crisps

Makes about 2-1/2 dozen. Serves 12.

2 T. butter, melted
8 10-inch flour tortillas
1/2 c. grated Parmesan cheese
1 egg white, beaten
Garnish: sesame, poppy and/or caraway seed
   onion powder, cayenne pepper or dried cumin

Brush butter lightly over one side of each tortilla;
sprinkle evenly with cheese and press down lightly.
Carefully turn tortillas over. Brush other side with egg
white and sprinkle with desired seeds and seasoning.
Cut each tortilla into 4 strips with a pastry cutter or knife.
Place strips cheese-side down on a baking sheet sprayed
with non-stick vegetable spray. Bake at 400 degrees, on
middle rack of oven, for 8 to 10 minutes, until crisp and
golden. Cool on a wire rack.

Nutrition Per Serving: 121 calories, 4g total fat, 2g sat fat,
7mg cholesterol, 250mg sodium, 15g carbohydrate, 0g fiber,
6g protein

Maple-Glazed Frankies

Maple-Glazed Frankies

Makes about 3-1/2 dozen. Serves 14.

1 t. butter
1 T. reduced-sodium soy sauce
1/4 c. pure maple syrup
14-oz. pkg. turkey cocktail wieners

In a saucepan over medium-low heat, stir together butter, soy sauce and maple syrup until slightly thickened. Add wieners and heat through.

Nutrition Per Serving: 62 calories, 3g total fat, 1g sat fat, 20mg cholesterol, 304mg sodium, 6g carbohydrate, 0g fiber, 5g protein

Simple Tomato Bruschetta

Serves 6.

4 to 5 plum tomatoes, chopped
1/4 c. red onion, diced
1 clove garlic, minced
1 T. olive oil
1 t. dried oregano
1 whole-grain baguette, sliced and toasted

Place tomatoes in a large bowl with a lid. Add onion, garlic, oil and oregano; toss to mix. Cover and refrigerate for 30 minutes to allow flavors to blend. To serve, spoon onto toasted baguette slices.

Nutrition Per Serving: 94 calories, 3g total fat, 0g sat fat, 0mg cholesterol, 122mg sodium, 14g carbohydrate, 3g fiber, 5g protein

Simple Tomato Bruschetta

Cinnamon-Almond Granola

Cinnamon-Almond Granola

Makes about 8 cups. Serves 16.

5-1/2 c. long-cooking oats, uncooked
1/2 c. sliced almonds
1/2 c. roasted unsalted sunflower kernels
1/2 c. sweetened flaked coconut
1/2 c. honey
1/4 c. butter, melted
1 t. cinnamon
1 t. almond extract

In a large bowl, mix together oats, almonds, sunflower kernels and coconut. In a separate bowl, stir together remaining ingredients. Pour honey mixture over oat mixture; stir until well mixed. Divide mixture between 2 lightly greased 15"x10" jelly-roll pans, spreading as evenly and thinly as possible. Bake, uncovered, at 200 degrees for 20 minutes; stir well and return to oven. Repeat steps 2 times, until lightly toasted and golden. Let cool completely; store in an airtight container for up to 2 weeks.

Nutrition Per Serving: *227 calories, 10g total fat, 4g sat fat, 8mg cholesterol, 50mg sodium, 30g carbohydrate, 4g fiber, 5g protein*

Quick tip

Make a good thing even better...sprinkle with toasted coconut you make yourself. Spread sweetened flaked coconut in a shallow pan and bake at 350 degrees for 7 to 12 minutes, stirring frequently, until toasted and golden.

Almond-Toffee Popcorn

Almond-Toffee Popcorn

Makes about 12 cups. Serves 12.

12 c. popped popcorn
3/4 c. sugar
1/2 c. butter
1/4 c. light corn syrup
1/4 c. water
1/2 c. chopped almonds, toasted
1/2 t. vanilla extract

Place popcorn in a large heat-proof bowl; remove any unpopped kernels and discard. In a large saucepan, combine remaining ingredients except vanilla. Cook over medium-high heat, stirring occasionally, until mixture reaches the soft-crack stage, or 270 to 289 degrees on a candy thermometer. Remove from heat; add vanilla and stir well. Pour over popcorn, mixing until coated. Spread on wax paper to dry.

Nutrition Per Serving: *196 calories, 10g total fat, 6g sat fat, 20mg cholesterol, 62mg sodium, 24g carbohydrate, 2g fiber, 2g protein*

Garden Patch Grilled Vegetables

Serves 10.

6 small onions, sliced into wedges
4 to 5 thin carrots, peeled
4 potatoes, sliced into wedges
1 red pepper, sliced into strips
1 green pepper, sliced into strips
1 to 2 zucchini, sliced lengthwise
1/4 lb. mushrooms
1/4 c. olive oil
1/4 c. fresh thyme, chopped
salt and pepper to taste

Cover onions, carrots and potatoes with water in a large saucepan. Simmer over medium-high heat until crisp-tender, about 15 to 20 minutes. Drain; cool slightly. Combine cooked and uncooked vegetables in a large bowl. Whisk together oil and thyme; drizzle half of mixture over vegetables. Arrange vegetables on a lightly oiled grill over medium-high heat. Grill until tender, turning often and brushing with remaining oil mixture. Sprinkle with salt and pepper to taste; serve warm.

Nutrition Per Serving: *123 calories, 6g total fat, 1g sat fat, 0mg cholesterol, 26mg sodium, 17g carbohydrate, 4g fiber, 3g protein*

Garden Patch
Grilled Vegetables

Island Fruit Salsa & Cinnamon Crisps

Cinnamon Crisps

Makes about 2-1/2 dozen. Serves 8.

1/2 t. vanilla extract
1 T. hot water
1/2 t. cinnamon
3 T. sugar
4 6-inch flour tortillas, each cut into 8 wedges

Combine vanilla and water in a cup; blend cinnamon and sugar in a separate cup. Brush vanilla mixture over both sides of tortilla wedges; sprinkle with cinnamon-sugar. Place on a baking sheet sprayed with non-stick vegetable spray. Bake at 450 degrees for 5 minutes, until crisp.

Nutrition Per Serving: 70 calories, 1g total fat, 0g sat fat, 0mg cholesterol, 102mg sodium, 14g carbohydrate, 0g fiber, 2g protein

Island Fruit Salsa & Cinnamon Crisps

Makes about 4-1/2 cups. Serves 8.

1 c. pineapple, peeled and diced
1 c. mango, peeled and diced
2/3 c. kiwi fruit, peeled and diced
1/2 c. yellow pepper, diced
1/2 c. red pepper, diced
1/2 c. red onion, finely chopped
1/4 c. fresh cilantro, chopped
1 t. lime juice
salt and pepper to taste

Combine all ingredients in a serving bowl. Chill for one hour to allow flavors to blend.

Nutrition Per Serving: 68 calories, 1g total fat, 0g sat fat, 0mg cholesterol, 2mg sodium, 17g carbohydrate, 3g fiber, 1g protein

Spicy Broccomole

Makes about 3 cups. Serves 10.

3 c. fresh or frozen broccoli flowerettes
1 jalapeño pepper, roasted, seeded and chopped
1 green onion, chopped
1/3 c. non-fat plain Greek yogurt
3 T. fresh cilantro, chopped
1 t. olive oil
1/4 t. chili powder
1/4 t. garlic powder
1/4 t. salt
1/4 t. pepper

In a saucepan over medium-high heat, cook broccoli in salted water until very soft. Drain well, squeezing out water with a paper towel. Transfer broccoli to a food processor or blender; add remaining ingredients. Process until smooth. If a smoother texture is desired, add a little more olive oil. Serve warm.

Nutrition Per Serving: 29 calories, 1g total fat, 0g sat fat, 1mg cholesterol, 87mg sodium, 3g carbohydrate, 1g fiber, 2g protein

Crab-Stuffed Mushrooms

Remove and chop mushroom stems, setting aside mushroom caps. Combine chopped stems with crabmeat, bread, egg, onion and seasonings; mix well. Spoon mixture into mushroom caps; sprinkle with cheese and set aside. Brush melted butter over a 13"x 9" baking pan; arrange mushroom caps in pan. Broil for 2 to 4 minutes, until golden and heated through.

Nutrition Per Serving: *41 calories, 2g total fat, 1g sat fat, 31mg cholesterol, 117mg sodium, 1g carbohydrate, 0g fiber, 3g protein*

Grilled Shrimp
Serves 6.

24 uncooked large shrimp, peeled and cleaned
1 onion, chopped
5 cloves garlic, diced
1/4 c. fresh parsley, chopped
8 leaves fresh basil, chopped
1 t. dry mustard
1 t. hot pepper sauce
1 t. salt
juice of 2 lemons
1/3 c. olive oil
6 wooden skewers, soaked in water

Place shrimp in a large plastic zipping bag. Mix remaining ingredients together; pour over shrimp. Seal bag and refrigerate for 24 hours, turning bag several times to coat shrimp with marinade. Drain and discard marinade; place 4 to 6 shrimp on each skewer. Place on a medium-high grill over hot coals. Grill for 4 to 8 minutes until slightly brownish pink; do not overcook. Serve warm.

Nutrition Per Serving: *82 calories, 6g total fat, 1g sat fat, 43mg cholesterol, 240mg sodium, 0g carbohydrate, 0g fiber, 6g protein*

Crab-Stuffed Mushrooms
Serves 15.

15 mushrooms
7-oz. can crabmeat, drained and flaked
1 slice whole-grain bread, torn
1 egg, beaten
1/3 c. onion, chopped
salt and pepper to taste
2 T. grated Parmesan cheese
2 T. butter, melted

Grilled Shrimp

Classic Starters & Snacks

Beef Fajita Skewers

Serves 8.

1 lb. boneless beef top sirloin, sliced into 1-inch cubes
8 wooden skewers, soaked in water
1 green pepper, cut into wedges
1 red or yellow pepper, cut into wedges
2 onions, cut into wedges
3 T. lime juice
1/3 c. low-calorie Italian salad dressing
salt to taste

Thread beef cubes onto 4 skewers; thread peppers and onions onto remaining skewers. Combine lime juice and salad dressing; brush over skewers. Grill over hot coals or on a medium-hot grill, turning occasionally, 7 to 9 minutes for beef and 12 to 15 minutes for vegetables. Sprinkle with salt to taste.

Nutrition Per Serving: 188 calories, 12g total fat, 4g sat fat, 47mg cholesterol, 206mg sodium, 3g carbohydrate, 1g fiber, 17g protein

Beef Fajita Skewers

Cheesy Spinach-Stuffed Mushrooms

Serves 12.

10-oz. pkg. frozen chopped spinach, thawed and squeezed dry
1/4 c. low-fat cream cheese, softened
1 c. crumbled reduced-fat feta cheese
3/4 t. garlic powder
1/4 t. pepper
24 mushrooms, stems removed
1/2 c. grated Parmesan cheese

In a bowl, combine all ingredients except mushroom caps and Parmesan cheese; mix well. Spoon mixture into mushrooms; place on a rimmed baking sheet. Sprinkle mushrooms with Parmesan cheese. Bake at 350 degrees for 15 to 20 minutes, until bubbly and heated through. Serve warm.

Nutrition Per Serving: 61 calories, 3g total fat, 2g sat fat, 12mg cholesterol, 192mg sodium, 1g carbohydrate, 1g fiber, 4g protein

Traditional Hummus

Makes about 2 cups. Serves 8.

2 15-oz. cans garbanzo beans, drained and rinsed
1/2 c. warm water
3 T. lime or lemon juice
1 T. tahini sesame seed paste
1-1/2 t. ground cumin
1 T. garlic, minced
1 t. salt

Place all ingredients in a food processor or blender. Process until very smooth, about 4 minutes. If a thinner consistency is desired, add an extra tablespoon or two of water. Transfer to a serving bowl.

Nutrition Per Serving: 111 calories, 2g total fat, 0g sat fat, 0mg cholesterol, 648mg sodium, 17g carbohydrate, 5g fiber, 6g protein

Cucumber Bites

Pinwheel Starters

Makes about 3 dozen. Serves 12.

8-oz. pkg. low-fat cream cheese, softened
2 T. light ranch dressing
3 12-inch wheat or spinach tortillas
3/4 c. Kalamata olives, chopped
1 c. carrots, peeled and shredded

Mix together cream cheese and ranch dressing. Spread cream cheese mixture evenly over one side of each tortilla. Stir together olives and carrots. Spoon over cream cheese mixture. Roll up each tortilla jelly-roll style; wrap each in plastic wrap. Chill for at least 2 hours; cut into one-inch slices.

Nutrition Per Serving: *127 calories, 8g total fat, 2g sat fat, 10mg cholesterol, 418mg sodium, 12g carbohydrate, 1g fiber, 3g protein*

Cucumber Bites

Makes 2 to 3 dozen. Serves 12.

2 cucumbers
5.2-oz. container light cream cheese spread with
  garlic & herbs
Garnish: thinly sliced smoked salmon, snipped
  fresh dill

Remove thin strips of peel from cucumbers with a potato peeler; slice 1/2-inch thick. Top each cucumber slice with one teaspoon cheese spread; garnish with salmon and dill. May be covered and chilled up to 3 hours before serving time.

Nutrition Per Serving: *35 calories, 2g total fat, 1g sat fat, 5mg cholesterol, 66mg sodium, 2g carbohydrate, 0g fiber, 2g protein*

Pinwheel Starters

Asian Chicken Wings

Asian Chicken Wings

Makes 2-1/2 to 3 dozen. Serves 12.

4 lbs. chicken wings
2 T. olive oil
1/2 t. salt
2 t. pepper, divided
1/4 c. honey
1 T. low-sodium soy sauce
1 t. low-sodium Worcestershire sauce
juice of 1 lime
zest of 2 limes
2 cloves garlic, finely minced
1 T. fresh cilantro, chopped
2 t. red pepper flakes

Place wings on an aluminum foil-lined 15"x10" jelly-roll pan. Drizzle wings with oil and toss to coat; sprinkle with salt and one teaspoon pepper. Bake at 400 degrees for 50 minutes; do not turn. Remove from oven. Using tongs, carefully lift wings from foil. Stir together pepper and other ingredients. Drizzle 1/3 cup of sauce mixture over hot wings and toss to coat. Serve remainder separately for dipping.

Nutrition Per Serving: *223 calories, 15g total fat, 4g sat fat, 63mg cholesterol, 201mg sodium, 6g carbohydrate, 0g fiber, 16g protein*

Shrimp-Stuffed Tomato Poppers

Serves 16.

2 pts. cherry tomatoes
1/2 lb. cooked shrimp, peeled and finely chopped
8-oz. pkg. light cream cheese, softened
1/4 c. light mayonnaise
1/4 c. grated Parmesan cheese
1 t. prepared horseradish
1 t. lemon juice
salt and pepper to taste
Garnish: chopped fresh parsley

Cut a thin slice off the top of each tomato; scoop out and discard pulp. Place tomatoes upside-down on a paper towel; let drain for 30 minutes. Combine remaining ingredients except parsley; blend until smooth. Spoon into tomatoes; sprinkle with parsley.

Nutrition Per Serving: *50 calories, 4g total fat, 3g sat fat, 28mg cholesterol, 207mg sodium, 3g carbohydrate, 0g fiber, 3g protein*

Avocado Feta Dip

Makes about 3 cups. Serves 12.

2 avocados, halved, pitted and diced
1 c. crumbled low-fat feta cheese
1 red pepper, diced
1 green onion, thinly sliced
1 T. lemon juice
2 t. dill weed
salt and pepper to taste

Combine all ingredients in a serving bowl; mix until smooth.

Nutrition Per Serving: *113 calories, 10g total fat, 1g sat fat, 7mg cholesterol, 111mg sodium, 4g carbohydrate, 1g fiber, 2g protein*

Shrimp-Stuffed Tomato Poppers

Classic Starters & Snacks

Special Deviled Eggs

Spicy Garlic Almonds

Makes about 3 cups. Serves 10.

2 T. low-sodium soy sauce
2 t. hot pepper sauce
2 cloves garlic, pressed
1 lb. blanched whole almonds
1 T. butter, melted
1 t. pepper
1/4 t. red pepper flakes

Combine sauces and garlic in a medium bowl. Add almonds, stirring until well coated. Brush butter over a 15"x10" jelly-roll pan. Spread almonds on pan in a single layer. Bake at 350 degrees for 10 minutes. Sprinkle salt and peppers over almonds; return to oven for 15 minutes. Remove from oven; cool on pan. Store in an airtight container.

Nutrition Per Serving: *282 calories, 24g total fat, 2g sat fat, 3mg cholesterol, 113mg sodium, 10g carbohydrate, 6g fiber, 11g protein*

Special Deviled Eggs

Makes 2 dozen. Serves 12.

1 doz. eggs, hard-boiled and peeled
3 to 4 T. reduced-fat coleslaw dressing
1/8 to 1/4 t. garlic salt with parsley
Garnish: paprika, snipped fresh chives

Slice eggs in half lengthwise; scoop yolks into a bowl. Arrange whites on a serving platter; set aside. Mash yolks well with a fork. Stir in dressing to desired consistency and add garlic salt to taste. Spoon or pipe yolk mixture into whites. Garnish as desired; chill.

Nutrition Per Serving: *79 calories, 5g total fat, 2g sat fat, 217mg cholesterol, 146mg sodium, 3g carbohydrate, 0g fiber, 6g protein*

Spicy Garlic Almonds

Chili Sweet Potato Fries

Serves 10.

3-1/2 lbs. sweet potatoes, sliced into 1-inch wedges
2 T. olive oil
3/4 t. salt
1/4 t. pepper
1/2 c. orange juice
1 T. honey
2 t. chili powder

Place potato wedges in a large plastic zipping bag; sprinkle with oil, salt and pepper. Toss to mix. Arrange potato wedges on lightly greased baking sheets. Stir together orange juice, honey and chili powder; set aside. Bake, uncovered, at 450 degrees for 25 to 30 minutes or until tender, shaking pans and basting with orange juice mixture several times.

Nutrition Per Serving: 195 calories, 3g total fat, 0g sat fat, 0mg cholesterol, 237mg sodium, 43g carbohydrate, 5g fiber, 3g protein

Chili Sweet Potato Fries

Teriyaki Chicken Skewers

Serves 6.

1/4 c. low-sodium soy sauce
1/4 c. brown sugar, packed
2 t. apricot jam
1/2 t. ground ginger
2 cloves garlic, pressed
2 boneless, skinless chicken breasts, cut into 1-inch cubes
8 green onions, cut into 1-inch lengths
6   8-inch skewers, soaked in water

Whisk together soy sauce, brown sugar, jam, ginger and garlic in a shallow bowl. Add chicken to sauce; toss to coat. Cover and refrigerate for one to 8 hours, stirring occasionally. Alternate chicken and onions on skewers, reserving marinade. Broil for 10 minutes, or until chicken is cooked through, turning several times and basting with reserved marinade. Discard any of the remaining marinade.

Nutrition Per Serving: 173 calories, 2g total fat, 0g sat fat, 24mg cholesterol, 451mg sodium, 22g carbohydrate, 0g fiber, 11g protein

Chapter

2

Garden-Fresh Salads & Satisfying Sides

(healthy goodness by the plateful)

Toss together taste and healthy goodness by making salads and sides that are packed with both flavor and nutrition. Fill up on Citrus & Beet Spinach Salad, enjoy a healthy helping of Mom's Macaroni & Cheese and ask for seconds of Comforting Creamed Corn. It feels good to know that you can enjoy every bite of these all-time-favorite, lightened-up recipes.

Gram's Zucchini in a Pan

Makes 6 servings.

1/4 c. olive oil
1 onion, thinly sliced and separated into rings
4 to 5 sweet Italian peppers, sliced
2 zucchini, thinly sliced
2 tomatoes, diced
1 t. Italian seasoning
salt and pepper to taste
3/4 c. low-fat shredded Cheddar cheese

Heat olive oil in a skillet over medium heat. Add onion and peppers; cover and cook until soft, about 5 minutes. Stir in zucchini, tomatoes and seasonings. Cover and cook to desired tenderness. Remove from heat; stir in cheese. Cover and let stand until cheese melts; serve warm.

Nutrition Per Serving: 121 calories, 10g total fat, 2g sat fat, 10mg cholesterol, 173mg sodium, 4g carbohydrate, 1g fiber, 5g protein

Herbed Mashed Potatoes

Serves 8.

6-1/2 c. potatoes, peeled and cubed
2 cloves garlic, halved
1/2 c. 2% milk
1/4 c. plain yogurt
1 T. butter, softened
2 T. fresh oregano, minced
1 T. fresh parsley, minced
1 T. fresh thyme, minced
3/4 t. salt
1/8 t. pepper

Place potatoes and garlic in a large saucepan; cover potatoes with water. Bring to a boil over medium-high heat. Reduce heat to medium; simmer for 20 minutes, or until potatoes are very tender. Drain; return potatoes and garlic to pan. Add remaining ingredients; beat with an electric mixer at medium speed to desired consistency.

Nutrition Per Serving: 94 calories, 1g total fat, 0g sat fat, 1mg cholesterol, 252mg sodium, 18g carbohydrate, 2g fiber, 4g protein

Comforting Creamed Corn

Makes 8 servings.

1 T. butter
4 c. corn, thawed if frozen
1/2 c. plain Greek yogurt
2 T. grated Parmesan cheese
1 t. dried basil

Melt butter in a non-stick skillet over medium heat; add corn. Cook for about 6 minutes, stirring occasionally, until tender. Reduce heat; stir in yogurt and cook for 4 minutes. Stir in cheese and basil just before serving.

Nutrition Per Serving: 88 calories, 2g total fat, 1g sat fat, 6mg cholesterol, 39mg sodium, 15g carbohydrate, 1g fiber, 4g protein

Quick tip

Freeze extra homemade broth in ice cube trays for terrific flavor when making rice. Broth ice cubes are also handy when whipping up gravies or sauces.

Comforting Creamed Corn

German Green Beans

Makes 6 servings.

2 14-1/2 oz. cans green beans, drained
15-1/4 oz. can corn, drained
1 t. seasoned salt
1 T. onion powder
1 clove garlic, minced
1 T. vinegar
4 to 5 T. olive oil
4 to 5 carrots, peeled and grated
1/2 t. dill weed
1/2 t. dried oregano
1/4 t. dried tarragon
3 slices bacon, crisply cooked and crumbled

In a large serving bowl, mix together all ingredients
except bacon. Cover and refrigerate overnight, stirring
occasionally. Top with bacon and serve at room
temperature.

Nutrition Per Serving: *210 calories, 13g total fat, 2g sat fat,
4mg cholesterol, 695mg sodium, 21g carbohydrate, 4g fiber,
4g protein*

German Green Beans

Spicy Roasted Potatoes

Makes 4 servings.

2 baking potatoes, cut into 1-inch cubes
1-1/2 t. dry mustard
1-1/2 t. Dijon mustard
1 t. olive oil
1 clove garlic, minced
1 t. dried tarragon
1/4 t. paprika
1/8 t. cayenne pepper

Place cubed potatoes in a bowl; set aside. In a separate
bowl, combine remaining ingredients; stir well and
pour over potatoes. Toss potatoes until well coated.
Arrange potatoes in a single layer on a lightly greased
baking sheet. Bake, uncovered, at 425 degrees for 30 to
35 minutes, until tender and golden.

Nutrition Per Serving: *57 calories, 1g total fat, 0g sat fat,
0mg cholesterol, 48mg sodium, 10g carbohydrate, 1g fiber,
1g protein*

Quick tip

It's easy to dry fresh herbs! Just bunch the
herbs together with kitchen twine and hang
upside-down in a cool, dry place.

Raspberry & Chicken Salad

Serves 6.

1 c. low-sodium chicken broth
1 c. water
4 boneless, skinless chicken breasts
1/3 c. olive oil
3 T. raspberry vinegar
1/2 t. Dijon mustard
salt and pepper to taste
10-oz. pkg. mixed salad greens
1 pt. raspberries

Combine chicken broth and water in a saucepan over medium heat. Cover; bring to a boil. Reduce heat and add chicken. Cover and simmer 10 minutes, or until cooked through; drain. Let chicken cool and cut into 1/4-inch slices. Combine olive oil, vinegar, mustard, salt and pepper in a small screw-top jar; shake well. In a large bowl, toss salad greens with 1/3 of dressing. In a blender, blend 1/3 cup of raspberries and remaining dressing until smooth. Arrange salad on individual serving plates; top with chicken and remaining raspberries. Drizzle with dressing; serve immediately.

Nutrition Per Serving: 239 calories, 14g total fat, 2g sat fat, 53mg cholesterol, 74mg sodium, 10g carbohydrate, 1g fiber, 19g protein

Raspberry & Chicken Salad

Arugula & Nectarine Salad

Arugula & Nectarine Salad

Makes 4 servings.

1/4 c. balsamic vinegar

1 T. Dijon mustard

1 T. honey

1/4 t. salt

pepper to taste

1/4 c. extra-virgin olive oil

1/4 lb. fresh arugula, torn

2 ripe nectarines, halved, pitted and sliced

3/4 c. chopped walnuts

1/2 c. crumbled feta cheese

Combine vinegar, mustard, honey, salt and pepper in a shaker jar. Add oil; shake until blended. Divide arugula among 4 salad plates; arrange nectarine slices over arugula. Sprinkle with walnuts and cheese; drizzle with salad dressing to taste.

Nutrition Per Serving: *376 calories, 32g total fat, 5g sat fat, 10mg cholesterol, 410mg sodium, 16g carbohydrate, 3g fiber, 7g protein*

Crunchy Apple-Pear Salad

Serves 6.

2 apples, cored and cubed

2 pears, cored and thinly sliced

1 T. lemon juice

2 heads butter lettuce, torn into bite-size pieces

1/2 c. low-fat crumbled gorgonzola cheese

1/3 c. canola oil

4 T. cider vinegar

1/4 c. sugar

1 t. celery seed

1/2 t. salt

1/4 t. pepper

1/2 c. chopped walnuts, toasted

Toss apples and pears with lemon juice; drain. Arrange lettuce on 6 salad plates; top with apples, pears and cheese. Combine remaining ingredients except walnuts in a jar with a tight-fitting lid. Cover; shake well until dressing is blended and sugar dissolves. Drizzle salad with dressing; sprinkle with walnuts. Serve immediately.

Nutrition Per Serving: *306 calories, 22g total fat, 3g sat fat, 7mg cholesterol, 332mg sodium, 25g carbohydrate, 5g fiber, 4g protein*

Micky's Crunchy Sweet-and-Sour Slaw

Makes 12 servings.

16-oz. pkg. shredded coleslaw mix

16-oz. pkg. shredded broccoli-carrot coleslaw mix

1-1/2 c. light mayonnaise

1/2 c. cider vinegar

1 t. garlic salt

pepper to taste

1 c. tomato, diced

Toss together coleslaw mixes in a serving bowl; set aside. In a small bowl, stir together remaining ingredients except tomato. Add to coleslaw mixture and toss to coat well. Gently fold in tomato. Serve immediately, or cover and refrigerate until serving time.

Nutrition Per Serving: *94 calories, 7g total fat, 1g sat fat, 10mg cholesterol, 459mg sodium, 6g carbohydrate, 2g fiber, 1g protein*

White Bean & Tomato Salad

Makes 6 servings.

15-oz. can cannellini beans, drained and rinsed
2 zucchini or yellow squash, diced
1 pt. cherry tomatoes, halved
1/2 c. red onion, chopped
3 T. olive oil
2 T. lemon juice
1/4 c. fresh cilantro, chopped

Combine all ingredients in a large bowl. Cover and refrigerate. Let stand at room temperature 20 to 30 minutes before serving.

Nutrition Per Serving: 128 calories, 7g total fat, 1g sat fat, 0mg cholesterol, 270mg sodium, 15g carbohydrate, 4g fiber, 5g protein

Jolene's Chickpea Medley

Makes 4 servings.

15-oz. can garbanzo beans, drained and rinsed
1 red pepper, diced
1 c. kale, finely shredded
1 zucchini, shredded
1 ear corn, kernels cut off, or 1/2 c. frozen corn, thawed
1/2 c. Italian salad dressing

In a salad bowl, combine beans and vegetables. Drizzle with salad dressing; toss to mix. Let stand 15 minutes before serving to allow flavors to blend.

Nutrition Per Serving: 244 calories, 13g total fat, 2g sat fat, 0mg cholesterol, 672mg sodium, 27g carbohydrate, 5g fiber, 6g protein

Mom's Macaroni & Cheese

Serves 6.

8-oz. pkg. multi-grain protein elbow macaroni, uncooked
5-oz. can evaporated milk
1 c. 2% milk
1/3 c. water
2 T. butter
3 T. all-purpose flour
1/2 t. salt
1 T. dried, minced onion
3/4 c. shredded sharp Cheddar cheese
1/2 c. shredded sharp low-fat Cheddar cheese
1/2 c. plain whole-grain panko bread crumbs
Garnish: chopped tomatoes, green onion

Cook macaroni according to package instructions; drain. Combine evaporated milk, milk and water; set aside. Melt butter in a medium saucepan over medium heat. Add flour and salt, whisking until blended. Add onion and evaporated milk mixture, stirring well to avoid lumps. Add cheese. Simmer until cheese melts and sauce is thickened, stirring frequently. Stir in macaroni. Pour into a lightly greased 8"x8" baking pan. Top with remaining low-fat cheese and panko. Bake, uncovered, at 350 degrees for 30 minutes, or until bubbly and lightly golden. Garnish with chopped tomatoes and green onion.

Nutrition Per Serving: 310 calories, 12g total fat, 8g sat fat, 36mg cholesterol, 441mg sodium, 39g carbohydrate, 4g fiber, 15g protein

Mom's Macaroni & Cheese

Spicy Cabbage-Apple Slaw

Spicy Cabbage-Apple Slaw

Makes 8 servings.

2 c. shredded green and red cabbage mix
2 c. apples, cored and chopped
1/2 c. celery, chopped
2 T. walnuts, chopped and toasted
2 T. golden raisins
1/2 c. low-fat plain yogurt
2 T. apple juice
1 T. honey
1/2 t. cinnamon

In a large serving bowl, combine cabbage mix, apples, celery, nuts and raisins; toss well. Combine remaining ingredients in a small bowl, stirring well. Pour yogurt mixture over cabbage mixture; toss well. Cover and chill for at least 30 minutes before serving.

Nutrition Per Serving: *65 calories,1g total fat, 0g sat fat, 0mg cholesterol, 33mg sodium, 11g carbohydrate, 2g fiber, 2g protein*

Quick tip

Kitchen shears are so handy for snipping fresh herbs, cutting stewed tomatoes right in the can and snipping the ends off fresh green beans. Just remember to wash them with soap and water after each use.

Rosemary-Braised Navy Beans

Makes 6 servings.

1 lb. dried navy beans
10 c. water
6 T. dried rosemary, divided
6 cloves garlic, divided
1-1/2 t. sea salt, divided
1/4 c. extra-virgin olive oil
1 roma tomato, diced
1/4 t. pepper to taste
1/4 c. fresh parsley, coarsely chopped

Cover beans with water; soak overnight. Drain; transfer to a Dutch oven. Add 10 cups water, 3 tablespoons rosemary, 3 pressed garlic cloves and one teaspoon salt. Bring to a boil over high heat. Reduce heat to medium-low; cover and simmer until beans are tender, about one hour. Drain, reserving cooking liquid. To beans in Dutch oven, add 1-1/2 cups reserved liquid, olive oil, tomato, pepper and remaining rosemary and salt. Slice remaining garlic and add to beans. Bake, uncovered, at 475 degrees for 15 to 20 minutes, until creamy. Add parsley and more of the cooking liquid if beans are too dry. Season with additional salt and pepper if desired.

Nutrition Per Serving: *349 calories, 10g total fat, 1g sat fat, 0mg cholesterol, 495mg sodium, 51g carbohydrate, 7g fiber, 20g protein*

Lemon-Garlic Brussels Sprouts

Makes 6 servings.

3 T. olive oil
2 lbs. Brussels sprouts, trimmed and halved
3 cloves garlic, minced
zest and juice of 1 lemon
sea salt and pepper to taste
3 T. Gruyère cheese, grated

Heat oil in a large skillet over medium-high heat. Add Brussels sprouts; sauté for 7 to 8 minutes. Turn sprouts over; sprinkle with garlic. Continue cooking 7 to 8 minutes, until sprouts are golden, caramelized and tender. Reduce heat to low. Add remaining ingredients except cheese; stir to combine. Adjust seasonings, if needed. Top with cheese just before serving.

Nutrition Per Serving: *95 calories, 4g total fat, 1g sat fat, 3mg cholesterol, 62mg sodium, 9g carbohydrate, 5g fiber, 7g protein*

Chicken Taco Salad

Makes 8 servings.

8 6-inch flour tortillas
2 c. cooked chicken breast, shredded
2 t. low-sodium taco seasoning
1/2 c. water
2 c. lettuce, shredded
1/2 c. low-sodium black beans, drained and rinsed
1 c. shredded low-fat Cheddar cheese
1/2 c. green onion, sliced
1/2 c. canned corn, drained
2-1/4 oz. can sliced black olives, drained
1/2 avocado, pitted, peeled and cubed
Garnish: fresh salsa

Microwave tortillas on high setting for one minute, or until softened. Press each tortilla into an ungreased muffin cup to form a bowl shape. Bake at 350 degrees for 10 minutes; cool. Combine chicken, taco seasoning and water in a skillet over medium heat. Cook, stirring frequently, until blended, about 5 minutes. Divide lettuce among tortilla bowls. Top with chicken and other ingredients, garnishing with salsa.

Nutrition Per Serving: *267 calories, 9g total fat, 1g sat fat, 25mg cholesterol, 538mg sodium, 31g carbohydrate, 2g fiber, 17g protein*

Lemon-Garlic Brussels Sprouts

Chicken Taco Salad

Apple-Pomegranate Salad
Makes 6 servings.

1 apple, peeled, cored and diced
juice of 1/2 lemon
1 head romaine lettuce, torn
seeds of 1 pomegranate
1/2 c. chopped pecans
2 T. champagne vinegar or white wine vinegar
2 T. canola oil
2 to 3 T. sugar
1/8 t. salt
1/2 c. shredded Parmesan cheese

In a small bowl, toss apple with lemon juice. Let stand for several minutes; rinse apple and pat dry. In a large serving bowl, combine apple, lettuce, pomegranate seeds and pecans. In a small jar, combine vinegar, oil, sugar and salt. Cover jar and shake thoroughly to mix; pour over salad. Toss until lettuce is completely coated; sprinkle with cheese.

Nutrition Per Serving: *216 calories, 14g total fat, 3g sat fat, 10mg cholesterol, 203mg sodium, 18g carbohydrate, 4g fiber, 6g protein*

Tomato Salad with Grilled Bread
Makes 8 servings.

3 lbs. tomatoes, cut into chunks
1 cucumber, peeled and sliced
4-oz. container crumbled feta cheese
1/4 c. balsamic vinegar
1/4 t. salt
1/4 t. pepper
8 thick slices crusty wheat bread, cubed
2 c. watermelon, cut into 1/2-inch cubes
1 red onion, very thinly sliced and separated into rings
3.8-oz. can sliced black olives, drained
1/4 c. plus 1/2 t. olive oil
1/2 c. fresh basil, torn

In a large serving bowl, combine tomatoes, cucumber, cheese, vinegar, salt and pepper. Toss to mix; cover and chill for one hour. Place bread cubes on an ungreased baking sheet. Bake at 350 degrees for 5 minutes, or until lightly golden. At serving time, combine tomato mixture with bread cubes and remaining ingredients. Toss very lightly and serve immediately.

Nutrition Per Serving: *268 calories, 13g total fat, 3g sat fat, 10mg cholesterol, 682mg sodium, 31g carbohydrate, 3g fiber, 8g protein*

Quick tip

For the healthiest meals, choose from a rainbow of colors...red beets, orange sweet potatoes, yellow summer squash, dark green kale and Brussels sprouts, purple eggplant and blueberries. Even white cauliflower offers valuable nutrients. So fill your plate and eat up!

Tomato Salad with Grilled Bread

Garden-Fresh Salads & Satisfying Sides

Sunflower Slaw

Serves 6.

1 head cabbage, shredded
5 carrots, peeled and shredded
1-1/2 c. fresh pineapple cubes
3-1/2 oz. pkg. unsalted roasted sunflower kernels
3/4 c. reduced-fat mayonnaise
2-1/2 T. lemon juice
2-1/2 T. orange juice

Combine cabbage, carrots, pineapple and sunflower kernels in a large bowl; toss well and set aside. Combine remaining ingredients in a small bowl, blending well. Pour over cabbage mixture and toss to coat. Chill before serving.

Nutrition Per Serving: 262 calories, 16g total fat, 2g sat fat, 10mg cholesterol, 346mg sodium, 25g carbohydrate, 7g fiber, 5g protein

Minted Tomato-Cucumber Salad

Makes 8 servings.

1/3 c. white balsamic vinegar
1 T. sugar
1/2 t. salt
pepper to taste
2 cucumbers, cubed
1 pt. cherry tomatoes, halved
1/2 c. red onion, chopped
1/2 c. fresh mint, chopped
2 T. olive oil

In a large serving bowl, stir together vinegar, sugar, salt and pepper. Add cucumbers; toss to coat. Cover and refrigerate for one hour, stirring occasionally. Add remaining ingredients; toss gently. Season with additional salt and pepper, if desired.

Nutrition Per Serving: 71 calories, 3g total fat, 0g sat fat, 0mg cholesterol, 151mg sodium, 8g carbohydrate, 1g fiber, 1g protein

Asian Summer Salad

Makes 8 servings.

8-oz. pkg. thin whole-grain spaghetti, uncooked and broken into fourths
3/4 c. carrot, peeled and cut into 2-inch strips
3/4 c. zucchini, cut into 2-inch strips
3/4 c. red pepper, chopped
1/3 c. green onion, sliced
3/4 lb. cooked chicken, cut into 2-inch-long strips
Garnish: chopped peanuts, chopped fresh cilantro

Cook pasta according to package directions; drain and rinse with cold water. In a bowl, combine all ingredients except garnish. Toss with Ginger Dressing. Refrigerate one hour; garnish as desired.

Ginger Dressing:
1/4 c. canola oil
3 T. rice vinegar
3 T. reduced-sodium soy sauce
2 t. sugar
1/8 t. fresh ginger, grated
1/8 t. cayenne pepper
1 clove garlic, chopped

Whisk together all ingredients.

Nutrition Per Serving: 217 calories, 9g total fat, 1g sat fat, 22mg cholesterol, 299mg sodium, 23g carbohydrate, 4g fiber, 13g protein

Asian Summer Salad

Scalloped Corn

Serves 6.

15-1/4 oz. can corn, drained
14-3/4 oz. can creamed corn
3/4 c. milk
1 egg, beaten
1 c. dry whole-wheat bread crumbs
1/4 c. onion, chopped
3 T. red pepper, chopped
salt and pepper to taste
1 T. butter
1 slice bacon, crisply cooked and crumbled

Combine first 3 ingredients; stir in egg. Add remaining ingredients except bacon and butter; pour into a lightly greased 1-1/2 quart casserole dish. Sprinkle with bacon; dot with butter. Bake, uncovered, at 350 degrees for 30 minutes.

Nutrition Per Serving: *220 calories, 5g total fat, 2g sat fat, 43mg cholesterol, 400mg sodium, 37g carbohydrate, 4g fiber, 7g protein*

Tomato-Basil Couscous Salad

Makes 6 servings.

2 c. water
1-1/2 c. couscous, uncooked
1 c. tomatoes, chopped
1/4 c. fresh basil, thinly sliced
1/2 c. olive oil
1/3 c. balsamic vinegar
1/2 t. salt
1/4 t. pepper

In a saucepan over high heat, bring water to a boil. Stir in uncooked couscous; remove from heat. Cover and let stand for 5 minutes, until water is absorbed. Add remaining ingredients and toss to mix. Cover and chill for several hours to overnight.

Nutrition Per Serving: *342 calories, 19g total fat, 3g sat fat, 0mg cholesterol, 203mg sodium, 38g carbohydrate, 3g fiber, 6g protein*

Scalloped Corn

Quick tip

Plant a vegetable garden with the kids! Even picky eaters may be willing to sample veggies that they grew themselves! Some easy-to-grow favorites are carrots, sweet peas, radishes, green beans and all kinds of peppers.

Tomato-Basil Couscous Salad

Garden-Fresh Salads & Satisfying Sides

Tomato & Mozzarella Salad
Makes 6 servings.

1 pt. cherry tomatoes, halved
8-oz. pkg. fresh mozzarella cheese, drained and
  cut into small pieces
1/2 c. fresh basil, sliced into thin strips
2 T. fresh parsley, snipped
1/4 c. lemon juice
3 T. olive oil
salt and pepper to taste
1 avocado, halved, pitted and diced

Combine tomatoes, cheese and herbs in a large salad
bowl; set aside. In a small bowl, whisk together lemon
juice, oil and seasonings. Pour over tomato mixture;
toss to coat. Cover and refrigerate for one hour. Stir in
avocado just before serving.

Nutrition Per Serving: 262 calories, 23g total fat, 6g sat fat,
20mg cholesterol, 289mg sodium, 6g carbohydrate, 2g fiber,
11g protein

Tomato & Mozzarella Salad

Quick tip
To preserve the beautiful color and tasty
flavor of beets, don't peel or slice them before
boiling. Simply trim off an inch of the stem and
root ends. After cooking, run the beets under
cold water and simply rub off the skins with a
paper towel.

Citrus & Beet Spinach Salad
Makes 8 servings.

10-oz. pkg. fresh baby spinach
2-1/2 c. beets, cooked, peeled and diced
2 oranges, sectioned and seeds removed
1/2 c. red onion, thinly sliced
1/3 c. chopped walnuts, toasted
1/2 c. raspberry vinaigrette salad dressing

In a large salad bowl, combine all ingredients except
salad dressing. Add salad dressing immediately before
serving; toss again and serve.

Nutrition Per Serving: 130 calories, 7g total fat, 1g sat fat,
0mg cholesterol, 282mg sodium, 15g carbohydrate, 4g fiber,
3g protein

Citrus & Beet Spinach Salad

Blueberry-Chicken Salad

Blueberry-Chicken Salad

Makes 4 servings.

2 c. chicken breast, cooked and cubed
3/4 c. celery, chopped
1/2 c. red pepper, diced
1/2 c. green onions, thinly sliced
2 c. blueberries, divided
6-oz. container lemon yogurt
3 T. light mayonnaise
1/2 t. salt
Garnish: Bibb lettuce

Combine chicken and vegetables in a large bowl. Gently stir in 1-1/2 cups blueberries; reserve remaining berries. In a separate bowl, blend remaining ingredients except lettuce. Drizzle over chicken mixture and gently toss to coat. Cover and refrigerate 30 minutes. Spoon salad onto lettuce-lined plates. Top with reserved blueberries.

Nutrition Per Serving: 190 calories, 5g total fat, 1g sat fat, 56mg cholesterol, 479mg sodium, 18g carbohydrate, 3g fiber, 16g protein

Seafood Salad for a Crowd

Serves 15.

3 8-oz. pkgs. cooked frozen shrimp, thawed
1 lb. imitation crabmeat, cut into bite-size pieces
5 cucumbers, peeled and diced
6 tomatoes, diced
1 bunch green onions, chopped
1 head lettuce, chopped
5 avocados, halved, pitted and diced
salt to taste
1/2 c. shredded low-fat Colby Jack cheese
1/2 c. light ranch salad dressing

In a large bowl, toss together all ingredients except cheese and salad dressing. Divide salad into individual bowls; top with cheese and salad dressing.

Nutrition Per Serving: 293 calories, 20g total fat, 3g sat fat, 107mg cholesterol, 580mg sodium, 14g carbohydrate, 4g fiber, 15g protein

Seafood Salad for a Crowd

Hot & Sweet Coleslaw

Makes 12 servings.

8 c. green cabbage, shredded
1 c. red cabbage, shredded
4 carrots, peeled and shredded
1 yellow onion, grated
1/2 c. low-fat mayonnaise
2 T. mustard
2 t. cider vinegar
1/4 c. sugar
1 t. pepper
1/4 t. cayenne pepper
salt and additional pepper to taste

In a large bowl, toss together vegetables. In a separate bowl, whisk together mayonnaise, mustard, vinegar, sugar and peppers. Toss mayonnaise mixture with cabbage mixture; season with salt and additional pepper, if desired. Cover and refrigerate overnight before serving.

Nutrition Per Serving: *83 calories, 2g total fat, 0g sat fat, 3mg cholesterol, 177mg sodium, 13g carbohydrate, 4g fiber, 2g protein*

Sunny Quinoa Salad

Serves 8.

2 c. quinoa, uncooked
2-1/2 c. low-sodium chicken broth
4 green onions, thinly sliced
1/2 c. golden raisins, chopped
2 T. rice vinegar
1/2 c. orange juice
1 t. orange zest
2 T. olive oil
1/4 t. ground cumin
1 cucumber, peeled and chopped
1/2 c. fresh flat-leaf parsley, chopped
salt and pepper to taste

Rinse quinoa under warm water for 3 minutes until water runs clear. In a saucepan, bring chicken broth to a boil. Add quinoa; return to a boil. Cover and simmer until quinoa has fully expanded, about 20 to 25 minutes. Remove from heat; fluff with a fork. In a large bowl, combine quinoa and remaining ingredients; mix well. Cover and chill before serving.

Nutrition Per Serving: *266 calories, 6g total fat, 1g sat fat, 0mg cholesterol, 156mg sodium, 42g carbohydrate, 4g fiber, 11g protein*

Hot & Sweet Coleslaw

Sunny Quinoa Salad

Penne with Healthy Vegetables

Penne with Healthy Vegetables

Serves 6.

16-oz. pkg. whole-wheat penne pasta, uncooked
1 lb. asparagus, cut into 1/2-inch pieces
1 carrot, thinly sliced
1/2 lb. sugar snap peas
3 T. olive oil
1/2 c. shredded Parmesan cheese
salt and pepper to taste

Cook pasta according to package directions. Add asparagus and carrots during the last 4 minutes of cook time; add peas during the last 2 minutes of cook time. Remove pot from heat; drain pasta mixture and return to pot. Toss with remaining ingredients; serve warm.

Nutrition Per Serving: *363 calories, 12g total fat, 2g sat fat, 5mg cholesterol, 98mg sodium, 57g carbohydrate, 11g fiber, 16g protein*

Layered Caribbean Chicken Salad

Layered Caribbean Chicken Salad

Makes 6 servings.

3 c. romaine lettuce, shredded
2 c. cooked chicken, cubed
1/2 c. shredded low-fat Monterey Jack cheese
15-1/2 oz. can black beans, drained and rinsed
1-1/2 c. mango, halved, pitted and cubed
1/2 c. plum tomatoes, chopped
1 c. shredded low-fat Cheddar cheese
1/2 c. green onions, thinly sliced
1/2 c. cashews, chopped

In a large clear glass serving bowl, layer all salad ingredients in order listed, except cashews. Spoon Dressing evenly over salad; sprinkle cashews over top.

Dressing:

6-oz. container low-fat piña colada yogurt
2 T. lime juice
1/2 t. Caribbean jerk seasoning

In a small bowl, mix all ingredients together until well blended.

Nutrition Per Serving: *430 calories, 11g total fat, 4g sat fat, 42mg cholesterol, 724mg sodium, 57g carbohydrate, 12g fiber, 33g protein*

Garden-Fresh Salads & Satisfying Sides

Sassy Squash
Serves 6.

1/2 c. red onion, thinly sliced
1 T. butter
3 c. yellow squash, thinly sliced
3 c. zucchini, thinly sliced
1 t. salt
pepper to taste
1 clove garlic, minced
16-oz. can stewed tomatoes

In a large skillet, sauté onion in butter over medium-high heat for 2 minutes. Stir in remaining ingredients except tomatoes. Reduce heat to medium and cook until crisp-tender. Add tomatoes and cook until heated through.

Nutrition Per Serving: 66 calories, 2g total fat, 1g sat fat, 5mg cholesterol, 589mg sodium, 9g carbohydrate, 3g fiber, 2g protein

Mexican Roasted Cauliflower
Makes 6 servings.

3 T. olive oil
3 cloves garlic, minced
1 T. chili powder, or to taste
1/2 t. ground cumin
1 lb. cauliflower, cut into bite-size flowerets
juice of 1 lime
1/4 c. fresh cilantro, chopped
salt to taste

Mix oil, garlic and spices in a large bowl. Add the cauliflower; toss to coat. Spread in an ungreased shallow roasting pan. Bake, uncovered, at 325 degrees for one hour and 15 minutes, stirring occasionally. Remove from oven. Drizzle with lime juice; sprinkle with cilantro and toss well. Serve warm.

Nutrition Per Serving: 123 calories, 7g total fat, 1g sat fat, 0mg cholesterol, 33mg sodium, 3g carbohydrate, 3g fiber, 3g protein

Sassy Squash

Mexican Roasted Cauliflower

Shrimp Tossed Salad

Serves 6.

1 head lettuce, torn
9-oz. pkg. fresh baby spinach
3 c. coleslaw mix
8-oz. can sliced water chestnuts, drained
1/3 c. golden raisins
1/3 c. sweetened dried cranberries
1/2 red pepper, very thinly sliced
2-lb. pkg. frozen cooked shrimp, thawed
1 carrot, peeled
1/2 c. chow mein noodles
Optional: chopped fresh dill
Garnish: sweet-and-sour salad dressing (2 T. per person)

In a large serving bowl, arrange half each of lettuce, spinach and coleslaw mix. Top with half each of water chestnuts, raisins and cranberries. Layer with remaining lettuce, spinach and coleslaw mix. Arrange red peppers around the edge of the salad. Arrange shrimp inside the pepper ring. Using a vegetable peeler, make carrot curls; arrange in center of bowl. Sprinkle with remaining water chestnuts, raisins and cranberries. Just before serving, top with chow mein noodles. If desired, sprinkle dill over the shrimp. Serve with salad dressing.

Nutrition Per Serving: *238 calories, 4g total fat, 1g sat fat, 321mg cholesterol, 818mg sodium, 28g carbohydrate, 9g fiber, 28g protein*

Tarragon Steak Dinner Salad

Serves 4.

6 c. Boston lettuce
2 pears, peeled, cored and sliced
1/2 red onion, thinly sliced
1/2 lb. grilled beef steak, thinly sliced
1/4 c. crumbled low-fat blue cheese
1/2 c. red wine vinaigrette salad dressing
1 T. fresh tarragon, minced
1/4 t. pepper

Arrange lettuce, pears and onion on 4 serving plates. Top with sliced steak and sprinkle with cheese. Combine dressing, tarragon and pepper in a small bowl; whisk well. Drizzle dressing mixture over salad.

Nutrition Per Serving: *313 calories, 15g total fat, 5g sat fat, 44mg cholesterol, 385mg sodium, 26g carbohydrate, 3g fiber, 19g protein*

Shrimp Tossed Salad

Tarragon Steak Dinner Salad

Candied Sweet Potatoes

Serves 8.

1/4 c. all-purpose flour
4 sweet potatoes, peeled and thinly sliced
1/4 c. brown sugar, packed
3 T. butter, sliced
2 T. maple-flavored pancake syrup
1/4 t. nutmeg

Shake flour in a large oven roasting bag; arrange bag in a 13"x9" baking pan. Toss sweet potatoes with remaining ingredients to blend; arrange in an even layer in bag. Close bag with nylon tie provided; cut six, 1/2-inch slits in top. Tuck ends of bag into pan. Bake at 350 degrees for 45 minutes.

Nutrition Per Serving: *211 calories, 4g total fat, 3g sat fat, 11mg cholesterol, 81mg sodium, 44g carbohydrate, 4g fiber, 2g protein*

Roasted Butternut Squash

Makes 4 servings.

4 c. butternut squash, halved and seeds removed
2 T. extra-virgin olive oil
1 T. fresh rosemary, snipped
2 t. kosher salt
1 t. pepper

Dice butternut squash and spread on an ungreased baking sheet. Drizzle with olive oil; add seasonings and toss with your hands. Bake, uncovered, at 400 degrees for 30 to 40 minutes, until tender and golden, stirring once. Season with additional salt and pepper, if desired.

Nutrition Per Serving: *126 calories, 5g total fat, 1g sat fat, 0mg cholesterol, 893mg sodium, 22g carbohydrate, 0g fiber, 2g protein*

Hearty Greek Salad

Makes 4 servings

2 c. lettuce, shredded
1 c. cherry tomatoes, halved
1 cucumber, diced
1 green pepper, diced
1 red onion, sliced
1/2 c. black or green olives, drained
1 T. red wine vinegar
2 T. lemon juice
3 T. extra-virgin olive oil
1/4 t. dried oregano
salt and pepper to taste
1/3 c. crumbled low-fat feta cheese

In a large serving bowl, combine lettuce, tomatoes, cucumbers, pepper, onion and olives. In a separate bowl, whisk together remaining ingredients except cheese. Pour dressing over lettuce mixture; toss well. Top with cheese and gently toss again.

Nutrition Per Serving: *193 calories, 15g total fat, 3g sat fat, 7mg cholesterol, 309mg sodium, 11g carbohydrate, 1g fiber, 3g protein*

Hearty Greek Salad

Emily's Frozen Fruit Salad

Emily's Frozen Fruit Salad

Makes 12 servings.

16-oz. can apricot halves in syrup
20-oz. can crushed pineapple in juice
1 c. fresh strawberries, sliced
6-oz. can frozen orange juice concentrate, thawed
1/2 c. water
3 bananas, sliced

Combine undrained apricots and pineapple. Mix in remaining ingredients except bananas. Prepare an 8"x8" baking pan by placing parchment paper in bottom and sides. Pour mixture into pan. Cover and freeze for at least 24 hours. Before serving, let stand at room temperature for about 15 minutes. Cut into rectangles to serve. Serve with banana slices.

Nutrition Per Serving: 86 calories, 0g total fat, 0g sat fat, 0mg cholesterol, 7mg sodium, 21g carbohydrate, 2g fiber, 1g protein

Black Cherry & Cranberry Salad

Makes 8 servings.

8-oz. can crushed pineapple in juice
1/4 c. water
.3-oz. pkg. sugar-free black cherry gelatin mix
16-oz. can whole-berry cranberry sauce
1 c. celery, chopped
1 c. chopped walnuts
1/4 c. lemon juice

In a saucepan over medium heat, mix undrained pineapple and water. Heat to boiling; add gelatin mix and stir until gelatin is dissolved. Add remaining ingredients and stir well. Transfer to a 6-cup serving dish. Chill in refrigerator for 4 hours, or until firm.

Nutrition Per Serving: 258 calories, 10g total fat, 1g sat fat, 0mg cholesterol, 392mg sodium, 27g carbohydrate, 3g fiber, 8g protein

Black Cherry & Cranberry Salad

Dilled New Potato Salad

Serves 8.

2 lbs. redskin potatoes, cut into wedges
10-oz. pkg. frozen petite sweet peas
1/2 c. light mayonnaise
1/2 c. plain yogurt
1 sweet onion, chopped
1/2 t. garlic salt
1/4 t. pepper
3 T. fresh dill, minced
1 T. Dijon mustard

In a saucepan over medium-high heat, cover potatoes with water. Cook for 15 minutes, or until nearly tender. Add peas and cook for an additional 2 minutes. Drain potatoes and peas. Cool slightly. In a large bowl, stir together remaining ingredients. Add potato mixture; toss gently to coat. Cover and chill at least 2 hours.

Nutrition Per Serving: 159 calories, 4g total fat, 1g sat fat, 5mg cholesterol, 381mg sodium, 25g carbohydrate, 4g fiber, 5g protein

Dilled New Potato Salad

Skillet-Toasted Corn Salad

Skillet-Toasted Corn Salad

Makes 8 servings.

1/3 c. plus 1 T. olive oil, divided
1/3 c. lemon juice
1 T. Worcestershire sauce
3 to 4 dashes hot pepper sauce
3 cloves garlic, minced
1/4 t. salt
1/2 t. pepper
6 ears sweet corn, husked and kernels removed
4 red, yellow and/or green peppers, coarsely chopped
1/2 c. shredded Parmesan cheese
1 head romaine lettuce, cut crosswise into 1-inch pieces

In a jar with a tight-fitting lid, combine 1/3 cup oil, lemon juice, sauces, garlic, salt and pepper. Cover and shake well; set aside. Heat remaining oil in a large skillet over medium-high heat. Add corn; sauté for 5 minutes, or until corn is tender and golden, stirring often. Remove from heat; keep warm. Combine corn, peppers and cheese in a large bowl. Pour olive oil mixture over top; toss lightly to coat. Serve over lettuce.

Nutrition Per Serving: 179 calories, 12g total fat, 3g sat fat, 8mg cholesterol, 204mg sodium, 16g carbohydrate, 3g fiber, 6g protein

Chapter 3

Family Favorite Entrees

(good-for-you main dishes)

Gather the family together for some comfort food that will make them feel good all day long. Get fired up for dinner with a Savory Zucchini Frittata, satisfy that craving for some healthy protein with Good & Healthy "Fried" Chicken and freshen up your table with colorful, vitamin-rich Super-Easy Stuffed Peppers. There's no worries about eating healthy when you choose these yummy main-dish meals.

Mom's Spaghetti & Meatballs

Serves 6.

2 8-oz. cans no-salt tomato sauce
1/2 t. garlic powder
1/2 t. dried oregano
1/2 t. dried basil
salt and pepper to taste
1 T. canola oil
16-oz. pkg. whole-grain spaghetti, cooked, or blanched
  spiralized or shaved zucchini
Garnish: shredded Parmesan cheese

In a large skillet over medium-low heat, combine tomato sauce and seasonings. Bring to a simmer. Meanwhile, make Meatballs. Add oil to skillet and brown meatballs. Add meatballs to sauce and simmer over medium-low heat for about 30 minutes, turning occasionally, until meatballs are no longer pink in the center. Serve sauce and meatballs over spaghetti or zucchini. Garnish with Parmesan cheese.

Meatballs:

1 lb. lean ground beef
3 T. shredded Parmesan cheese
2 eggs, beaten
1 slice white bread, crumbled
1/2 t. garlic salt

Combine all ingredients in a large bowl; mix well. Form into 2-inch balls.

Nutrition Per Serving with wheat pasta: *512 calories, 20g total fat, 3g sat fat, 124mg cholesterol, 367mg sodium, 59g carbohydrate, 9g fiber, 29g protein*

Nutrition Per Serving with zucchini: *275 calories, 18g total fat, 3g sat fat, 124mg cholesterol, 367mg sodium, 8g carbohydrate, 1g fiber, 18g protein*

Mom's Spaghetti & Meatballs with Pasta

Chicken & Peppers Stir-Fry

Serves 4.

1/4 c. low-sodium soy sauce
1 T. sesame oil
1 T. catsup
3 cloves garlic, minced
4 boneless, skinless chicken breasts, cut into 1-inch pieces
1/2 red pepper, chopped
1/2 yellow pepper, chopped
2 c. cooked brown rice

In a bowl, whisk together soy sauce, oil, catsup and garlic. Heat mixture in a skillet over medium-high heat. Add chicken; cook and stir for 3 minutes. Add peppers; cook and stir 5 minutes, or until chicken is cooked through. Serve over hot rice.

Nutrition Per Serving: *291 calories, 7g total fat, 1g sat fat, 80mg cholesterol, 613mg sodium, 26g carbohydrate, 2g fiber, 31g protein*

Mom's Spaghetti & Meatballs
with Zucchini

BBQ Pork Ribs

Serves 6.

3 qts. water
4 lbs. pork ribs, cut into serving-size portions
1 onion, quartered
1 t. salt
1/4 t. pepper

Bring water to a boil in a large stockpot over high heat. Add ribs, onion, salt and pepper. Reduce heat; cover and simmer for 1-1/2 hours. Remove ribs from pot; drain. Grill ribs for 10 minutes on each side, brushing frequently with BBQ Sauce, until tender.

BBQ Sauce:

1/2 c. vinegar
1 T. lemon juice
1/2 c. chili sauce
1/4 c. low-sodium Worcestershire sauce
2 T. onion, chopped
1/2 c. brown sugar, packed
1/2 t. dry mustard
1/8 t. garlic powder
1/8 t. cayenne pepper

Combine all ingredients in a small saucepan. Simmer over low heat for one hour, stirring frequently.

Nutrition Per Serving: 644 calories, 36g total fat, 12g sat fat, 219mg cholesterol, 537mg sodium, 22g carbohydrate, 0g fiber, 56g protein

Picture-Perfect Paella

Serves 8.

3 lbs. chicken
2 onions, quartered
1 stalk celery, sliced
2 carrots, peeled and sliced
salt and pepper to taste
6 c. water
2 c. long-cooking rice, uncooked
2 cloves garlic, crushed
1/4 c. oil
1 c. peas
1/4 c. diced pimentos, drained
1/2 t. dried oregano
1/8 t. saffron or turmeric
1 lb. uncooked large shrimp, peeled and cleaned
12 uncooked clams in shells

In a large skillet over medium heat, combine chicken pieces, onions, celery, carrots, salt, pepper and water. Bring to a boil; reduce heat, cover and simmer for one hour. Remove vegetables and chicken, reserving 6 cups broth. Dice chicken and set meat aside, discarding bones. In the same skillet over medium heat, cook and stir rice and garlic in oil until golden. Add reserved chicken, reserved broth, peas, pimentos, oregano and saffron or turmeric. Cover and cook over low heat for 15 minutes. Add shrimp and clams; cover and cook for another 10 minutes, or until shrimp are pink and clams have opened.

Nutrition Per Serving: 489 calories, 11g total fat, 1g sat fat, 196mg cholesterol, 536mg sodium, 42g carbohydrate, 2g fiber, 52g protein

Picture-Perfect Paella

Italian Sausage Skillet

Serves 6.

1-1/4 lb. pkg. Italian turkey sausage links
3 zucchini, cubed
1/2 c. onion, chopped
14-1/2 oz. can no-salt stewed tomatoes
3 c. cooked whole-grain pasta

In a skillet over medium heat, cook sausage until no longer pink; drain. Cut sausage into 1/4-inch slices; return to skillet and cook until browned. Add zucchini and onion; cook and stir for 2 minutes. Stir in tomatoes with juice. Reduce heat; cover and simmer for 10 to 15 minutes, until zucchini is tender. Serve mixture over cooked pasta.

Nutrition Per Serving: *341 calories, 10g total fat, 3g sat fat, 65mg cholesterol, 1053mg sodium, 47g carbohydrate, 7g fiber, 23g protein*

Italian Sausage Skillet

Super-Easy Stuffed Peppers

Serves 4.

4 green, red or orange peppers, tops removed, reserving if desired
1 lb. ground beef
1 onion, diced
1 T. Italian seasoning
1 clove garlic, pressed
3 c. cooked brown rice
26-oz. can spaghetti sauce, divided
salt and pepper to taste
Garnish: grated Parmesan cheese

Bring a large saucepan of water to a boil; add peppers and boil until tender. Drain and set aside. Brown ground beef with onion in a skillet; drain. Add Italian seasoning and garlic. Set aside 1/2 cup spaghetti sauce. Combine ground beef mixture, remaining sauce, cooked rice, salt and pepper in a bowl. Arrange peppers in a lightly greased 8"x8" baking pan. Fill peppers completely with ground beef mixture, spooning any extra mixture between peppers. Top with reserved sauce. Add pepper tops if using. Lightly cover with aluminum foil; bake at 400 degrees for 20 to 25 minutes. Sprinkle with Parmesan cheese.

Nutrition Per Serving: *579 calories, 24g total fat, 3g sat fat, 78mg cholesterol, 538mg sodium, 78g carbohydrate, 10g fiber, 29g protein*

Quick tip

It is so much easier to slice uncooked meat for stir-frying when it is slightly frozen...pop it in the freezer for 10 to 15 minutes before slicing.

Super-Easy Stuffed Peppers

Good & Healthy "Fried" Chicken

Good & Healthy "Fried" Chicken

Makes 5 servings.

1 c. whole-grain panko bread crumbs
1 c. cornmeal
2 T. all-purpose flour
salt and pepper to taste
1 c. buttermilk
10 chicken legs

Combine panko, cornmeal, flour, salt and pepper in a gallon-size plastic zipping bag. Coat chicken with buttermilk, one piece at a time. Drop chicken into bag and shake to coat pieces lightly. Arrange chicken on baking pan coated with non-stick vegetable spray. Bake, uncovered, at 350 degrees for 40 to 50 minutes, until chicken juices run clear.

Nutrition Per Serving: 285 calories, 8g total fat, 2g sat fat, 69mg cholesterol, 147mg sodium, 32g carbohydrate, 1g fiber, 21g protein

Ham & Feta Cheese Omelet

Makes one serving.

2 eggs, beaten
1/4 c. low-fat crumbled feta cheese
1/4 c. cucumber, diced
1 T. green onion, chopped
1/4 c. cooked ham, cubed
1/3 c. sliced black olives
salt and pepper to taste
Garnish: salsa

Combine all ingredients except salsa in a bowl; mix well. Pour into a lightly greased sauté pan or small skillet. Without stirring, cook over low heat until set. Fold over; transfer to serving plate. Serve with salsa.

Nutrition Per Serving: 339 calories, 19g total fat, 7g sat fat, 483mg cholesterol, 636mg sodium, 8g carbohydrate, 0g fiber, 27g protein

Barbecue Chicken Kabobs

Serves 6.

4 boneless, skinless chicken breasts, cubed
1 green pepper, cut into 2-inch squares
1 sweet onion, cut into wedges
1 red pepper, cut into 2-inch squares
1 c. favorite low-sodium barbecue sauce
6 skewers

Thread chicken, green pepper, onion and red pepper pieces alternately onto skewers. Place kabobs on a lightly oiled grill pan over medium heat. Cook for 12 to 15 minutes, turning and brushing frequently with barbecue sauce, until chicken juices run clear and vegetables are tender.

Nutrition Per Serving: 177 calories, 2g total fat, 0g sat fat, 53mg cholesterol, 329mg sodium, 20g carbohydrate, 1g fiber, 17g protein

Barbecue Chicken Kabobs

Baked Shrimp & Grits

Baked Shrimp & Grits

Serves 6.

5 c. water
1-1/4 c. quick-cooking grits, uncooked
1 c. shredded low-fat Cheddar cheese
1/4 c. butter
2 eggs, beaten
1 c. milk
garlic powder and salt to taste
1 lb. uncooked medium shrimp, peeled and cleaned
2 T. olive oil
1/2 c. white wine
2 t. garlic, minced
1-1/2 t. fresh parsley, chopped
1/4 t. salt
1/2 t. pepper
4 T. lemon juice

Bring water to a boil in a saucepan over medium-high heat. Cook grits in boiling water for 5 minutes. Add cheese, butter, eggs, milk, garlic powder and salt to grits; mix well. Spoon into a greased 4-quart casserole dish. Bake, uncovered, at 350 degrees for 45 minutes, or until lightly golden. Meanwhile, in a skillet over medium heat, sauté shrimp in olive oil until cooked through. Add remaining ingredients; heat through. Top grits with shrimp mixture before serving.

Nutrition Per Serving: *276 calories, 15g total fat, 7g sat fat, 254mg cholesterol, 711mg sodium, 28g carbohydrate, 3g fiber, 24g protein*

Hungarian Goulash

Makes 10 servings.

2 lbs. stew beef, cubed
2 lbs. pork shoulder, cubed
1-1/2 to 2 c. vinegar
1/4 to 1/2 c. butter
2 t. paprika
1 t. salt
1/2 to 1 t. caraway seed
3 15-oz. cans stewed tomatoes
4 c. cooked medium egg noodles

Toss meat with vinegar in a large bowl just to coat. Remove and let stand for 5 to 10 minutes. Melt butter in a large stockpot; add meat and paprika. Brown lightly on all sides. Add salt, caraway seed and undrained tomatoes, one can at a time, just until meat is covered. Simmer over low heat for 1-1/2 hours, until meat is tender. Serve over egg noodles.

Nutrition Per Serving: *526 calories, 23g total fat, 10g sat fat, 174mg cholesterol, 693mg sodium, 22g carbohydrate, 3g fiber, 54g protein*

Hungarian Goulash

Golden Baked Pork Chops

Serves 8.

1/2 c. dry bread crumbs
1/4 c. grated Parmesan cheese
1 T. dried oregano
1 t. dried marjoram
2 eggs, beaten
3-1/2 lb. boneless center-cut pork roast, sliced
   into 8 chops
salt and pepper to taste

Mix bread crumbs, Parmesan cheese and herbs in a shallow bowl; set aside. Place eggs in a separate bowl. Dip pork chops into egg, then into crumb mixture, reserving any remaining crumb mixture. Place on a greased aluminum foil-lined baking sheet and bake for one hour or until done, adding salt and pepper to taste.

Nutrition Per Serving: *387 calories, 19g total fat, 8g sat fat, 182mg cholesterol, 196mg sodium, 5g carbohydrate, 0g fiber, 44g protein*

Favorite Chicken & Dumplings

Serves 6.

2 T. oil
1 c. celery, chopped
1 c. carrots, peeled and sliced
1 T. onion, chopped
49-oz. can low-sodium chicken broth
10-3/4 oz. can low-sodium cream of chicken soup
1/8 t. pepper
2 c. cooked chicken, cubed
1-2/3 c. reduced-salt biscuit baking mix
2/3 c. milk

Heat oil in a Dutch oven over medium-high heat. Sauté celery, carrots and onion in oil for about 7 minutes, until crisp-tender. Add broth, soup and pepper; bring to a boil. Reduce heat to low; stir in chicken and bring to a simmer. In a separate bowl, stir together baking mix and milk. Drop batter by tablespoonfuls into simmering broth. Cover and cook over low heat for 15 minutes without lifting lid.

Nutrition Per Serving: *305 calories, 10g total fat, 2g sat fat, 38mg cholesterol, 671mg sodium, 35g carbohydrate, 1g fiber, 21g protein*

Roast Chicken with Vegetables

Serves 6.

3-1/2 lb. chicken
1 T. plus 1 t. olive oil, divided
1 t. dried thyme
1/2 t. salt
1/2 t. pepper
4 medium white onions, quartered
10 multi-colored or regular baby carrots
6 stalks celery, cut into 2-inch pieces
4 redskin potatoes, peeled and quartered

Place chicken in a large shallow roasting pan. Tie the legs together with kitchen string; insert meat thermometer into thickest part of thigh without touching bone. Rub chicken with one teaspoon oil; sprinkle with thyme, salt and pepper. Bake, uncovered, at 475 degrees for 15 minutes. Toss vegetables with remaining oil; arrange around chicken. Reduce oven to 400 degrees; bake for an additional 35 to 45 minutes, until chicken's internal temperature reaches 170 degrees.

Nutrition Per Serving: *554 calories, 27g total fat, 6g sat fat, 112mg cholesterol, 217mg sodium, 41g carbohydrate, 5g fiber, 32g protein*

Roast Chicken with Vegetables

Sam's Sweet-and-Sour Pork

Serves 8.

1 T. oil
1 lb. boneless pork loin, cut into 1/2-inch cubes
1 c. onion, chopped
1 c. green pepper, cut into 3/4-inch cubes
1 c. red pepper, cut into 3/4-inch cubes
1 t. garlic, minced
8-oz. can pineapple chunks, drained
1 c. catsup
1 T. brown sugar, packed
1 T. white vinegar
1/2 t. salt
1/4 t. pepper
4 c. cooked brown rice

Heat oil in a large skillet over medium-high heat; brown pork on both sides. Add onion, peppers and garlic; cook and stir 5 minutes. Drain; add remaining ingredients except rice. Cover and simmer 10 minutes, or until pork is tender. Serve over hot rice.

Nutrition Per Serving: *255 calories, 6g total fat, 2g sat fat, 30mg cholesterol, 768mg sodium, 37g carbohydrate, 3g fiber, 16g protein*

Sam's Sweet-and-Sour Pork

Mom's Beef Stroganoff

Serves 4.

1/2 c. all-purpose flour
1 t. paprika
1 t. dry mustard
1 t. salt
1/2 t. pepper
1-1/2 lbs. stew beef, sliced into strips
2 T. olive oil
1 onion, thinly sliced
3/4 lb. sliced mushrooms
1 c. water
14-1/2 oz. can low-sodium beef broth
1/2 c. plain low-fat yogurt
8-oz. pkg. wide egg noodles, cooked
Garnish: paprika, dried parsley

Combine flour and seasonings in a large plastic zipping bag. Add beef; seal and shake until all the meat is coated. Remove meat; reserve flour in plastic zipping bag. Heat oil in a Dutch oven over medium heat; brown meat on all sides. Add onion and mushrooms; sauté. Sprinkle with reserved flour; stir to mix. Add water and broth; stir. Reduce heat; cook for about one hour, until sauce is thickened and meat is tender. Remove from heat; stir in yogurt. Do not boil. Place noodles in large serving dish; spoon meat mixture over noodles. Sprinkle with paprika and parsley.

Nutrition Per Serving: *600 calories, 16g total fat, 4g sat fat, 151mg cholesterol, 898mg sodium, 48g carbohydrate, 2g fiber, 64g protein*

Mom's Beef Stroganoff

Delicious Pot Roast

Serves 10.

4-lb. boneless beef chuck roast
2 cloves garlic, sliced
1/2 t. salt
1/2 t. pepper
1/4 c. all-purpose flour
2 T. olive oil
1 onion, sliced
1 c. low-sodium beef broth
8-oz. can no-salt tomato sauce
1 T. brown sugar, packed
1 t. dried oregano
1 t. prepared horseradish
1 t. mustard
1 bay leaf
8 new redskin potatoes
6 carrots, peeled and quartered
4 stalks celery, sliced

Cut small slits in the top of roast; insert a slice of garlic into each slit. Season with salt and pepper. Place flour in a bowl; dredge roast in flour. Heat oil in a Dutch oven over medium heat. Brown roast on both sides in oil. Add onion and broth. Combine tomato sauce, brown sugar and seasonings in a bowl; pour over roast. Bring to a boil; reduce heat, cover and simmer for 1-1/2 hours. Add remaining ingredients. Cover and cook for one hour. Discard bay leaf. Serve with sauce from Dutch oven over top.

Nutrition Per Serving: *606 calories, 35g total fat, 13g sat fat, 118mg cholesterol, 333mg sodium, 31g carbohydrate, 5g fiber, 39g protein*

Delicious
Pot Roast

Just Like Mom's Meatloaf

Serves 6.

2 eggs, beaten
8-oz. can no-salt tomato sauce
3/4 c. unsalted cracker crumbs
1/4 c. onion, chopped
1/4 c. green pepper, finely chopped
1 T. reduced-sodium Worcestershire sauce
1/2 t. salt
1/2 t. pepper
1-1/2 lbs. lean ground beef
1/2 c. low-sodium catsup
2 t. mustard
2 T. brown sugar, packed

Combine first 8 ingredients in a bowl; add ground beef and mix well. Shape into a loaf; place in an ungreased 9"x5" loaf pan. Bake, uncovered, at 350 degrees for one hour. Combine catsup, mustard and brown sugar; spoon over meatloaf and bake an additional 10 to 15 minutes.

Nutrition Per Serving: *369 calories, 22g total fat, 4g sat fat, 150mg cholesterol, 431mg sodium, 18g carbohydrate, 1g fiber, 24g protein*

Just Like Mom's
Meatloaf

Tuna Noodle Casserole

Serves 6.

16-oz. pkg. wide egg noodles, cooked
10-3/4 oz. can low-sodium cream of mushroom soup
6-oz. can tuna, drained
1 c. frozen peas, thawed
4-oz. can sliced mushrooms, drained
1 c. 2% milk
salt and pepper to taste
1 c. shredded low-fat Cheddar cheese

Combine noodles, soup, tuna, peas and mushrooms; stir in milk. Add salt and pepper to taste. Spread in a lightly greased 9"x9" baking pan; sprinkle with cheese. Bake, uncovered, at 350 degrees for 25 minutes, until hot and bubbly.

Nutrition Per Serving: *348 calories, 6g total fat, 2g sat fat, 98mg cholesterol, 807mg sodium, 51g carbohydrate, 3g fiber, 24g protein*

Peach Oatmeal Pancakes

Makes about one dozen. Serves 6.

1-2/3 c. reduced-sodium pancake mix
1 c. quick-cooking oats, uncooked
1/4 c. brown sugar, packed
1 T. cinnamon
2 egg whites, beaten
1 T. vanilla extract
1 peach, pitted, peeled and diced
Optional: 1/2 c. chopped nuts

In a large bowl, combine pancake mix, oats, brown sugar and cinnamon; mix well. Stir in remaining ingredients.

Pour batter by 1/4 cupfuls onto a hot buttered griddle. Turn pancakes when bubbles form and start to pop; cook other side until golden.

Nutrition Per Serving: *254 calories, 3g total fat, 0g sat fat, 0mg cholesterol, 504mg sodium, 43g carbohydrate, 1g fiber, 14g protein*

Savory Zucchini Frittata

Makes 6 servings.

2 T. olive oil
3 shallots, finely minced
3 cloves garlic, finely minced
6 zucchini, sliced 1/4-inch thick
1 doz. eggs, lightly beaten
salt and white pepper to taste
1 c. fresh Italian flat-leaf parsley, snipped
1/2 c. shredded Parmesan cheese

Add oil to a large oven-safe skillet over medium heat; swirl to coat bottom and sides of pan. Add shallots and garlic; cook and stir for about one minute. Add zucchini; cook, stirring often, for 5 to 7 minutes, until crisp-tender. Remove pan from heat; add remaining ingredients and mix lightly. Bake in skillet, uncovered, at 325 degrees until set, about 30 minutes. Serve warm.

Nutrition Per Serving: *261 calories, 18g total fat, 6g sat fat, 430mg cholesterol, 287mg sodium, 11g carbohydrate, 3g fiber, 26g protein*

Savory Zucchini Frittata

Chicken & Snow Pea Stir-Fry

Chicken & Snow Pea Stir-Fry

Makes 4 servings.

3/4 c. orange juice
3 T. low-sodium soy sauce
3 t. cornstarch
1 T. brown sugar, packed
1/2 t. ground ginger
1 lb. boneless, skinless chicken breast, thinly sliced
2 t. canola oil
14-1/2 oz. can diced tomatoes
2 c. snow peas, trimmed
2 c. cooked brown rice

In a small bowl, combine orange juice, soy sauce, cornstarch, brown sugar and ginger; mix well and set aside. In a wok or large skillet over medium-high heat, cook and stir chicken in oil for 2 minutes, or until golden. Drain; add orange juice mixture and tomatoes with juice to skillet. Cook and stir until mixture is thickened. Add snow peas; cook and stir for 2 minutes, or until crisp-tender. Serve chicken mixture over brown rice.

Nutrition Per Serving: 346 calories, 6g total fat, 0g sat fat, 80mg cholesterol, 591mg sodium, 41g carbohydrate, 5g fiber, 31g protein

Quick tip

Make a double batch of your favorite comfort food and invite neighbors over for supper. What a great way to get to know them better. Keep it simple with a tossed salad, warm bakery bread and apple crisp for dessert. It's all about food and fellowship!

Dijon Chicken with Herbs

Serves 6.

6 boneless, skinless chicken breasts
1 t. kosher salt
1 t. pepper
3 T. Dijon mustard
2 T. fresh rosemary, minced
2 T. fresh thyme, minced
2 T. fresh parsley, minced

Sprinkle chicken with salt and pepper. Grill over medium-high heat 5 to 6 minutes per side, or until juices run clear. Remove from grill and brush both sides with mustard; sprinkle with herbs.

Nutrition Per Serving: 147 calories, 3g total fat, 0g sat fat, 80mg cholesterol, 570mg sodium, 2g carbohydrate, 0g fiber, 26g protein

Dijon Chicken with Herbs

Creole Pork Chops & Rice

Makes 4 servings.

4 pork chops
1 T. oil
1 c. onion, diced
1 c. celery, diced
1 c. long-cooking rice, uncooked
29-oz. can no-salt tomato sauce
15-oz. can no-salt diced tomatoes
salt and pepper to taste

In a skillet over medium heat, cook pork chops in oil until golden but not cooked through. Add onion, celery and uncooked rice; stir in remaining ingredients. Reduce heat to low. Cover and simmer until rice is tender, about 15 to 20 minutes, adding water as needed to prevent drying out.

Nutrition Per Serving: 564 calories, 17g total fat, 5g sat fat, 106mg cholesterol, 304mg sodium, 56g carbohydrate, 6g fiber, 43g protein

Creole Pork Chops & Rice

Make-Ahead Brunch Casserole

Makes 8 servings.

1 T. butter
1 onion, chopped
1/4 c. red pepper, chopped
2 c. sliced mushrooms
4 c. frozen shredded hashbrowns, thawed
salt and pepper to taste
1/4 t. garlic salt
4 slices bacon, crisply cooked and crumbled
4 eggs
1-1/2 c. 2% milk
1/8 t. dried parsley
1/2 c. shredded low-fat Cheddar cheese

Melt butter in a skillet over medium heat. Sauté onion, pepper and mushrooms until tender; set aside. Spread hashbrowns in a greased 13"x9" baking pan. Sprinkle with salt, pepper and garlic salt; top with bacon, onion and mushrooms. Whisk together eggs with milk and parsley; pour over casserole and top with cheese. Cover and refrigerate overnight. Bake, uncovered, at 400 degrees for one hour, or until set.

Nutrition Per Serving: 157 calories, 7g total fat, 3g sat fat, 119mg cholesterol, 269mg sodium, 13g carbohydrate, 1g fiber, 11g protein

Quick tip

Take time to share family stories and traditions with your kids over the dinner table. A cherished family recipe can be a super conversation starter.

Make-Ahead
Brunch Casserole

Foil-Wrapped Baked Salmon

Serves 4.

4 salmon fillets
1 onion, sliced
1/4 c. butter, diced
1 lemon, thinly sliced
1/4 c. brown sugar, packed

Place each fillet on a piece of aluminum foil that has been sprayed with non-stick vegetable spray. Top fillets evenly with onion slices, diced butter, lemon slices and brown sugar. Fold over foil tightly to make packets; make several holes in top of packets with a fork to allow steam to escape. Arrange packets on an ungreased baking sheet. Bake at 375 degrees for 15 to 20 minutes.

Nutrition Per Serving: *491 calories, 26g total fat, 9g sat fat, 173mg cholesterol, 177mg sodium, 15g carbohydrate, 1g fiber, 46g protein*

Foil-Wrapped Baked Salmon

Chicken Cacciatore

Makes 6 servings.

3 lbs. chicken, skin removed
1/2 c. all-purpose flour
3 T. olive oil
1 c. onion, thinly sliced
1/2 c. green pepper, sliced
1 clove garlic, minced
1/4 c. low-sodium chicken broth
15-oz. can diced tomatoes, drained
8-oz. can tomato sauce
4-oz. can sliced mushrooms, drained
1/4 t. dried oregano
1/2 t. salt

Pat chicken pieces dry; coat with flour. In a large skillet, heat oil over medium heat. Place chicken in skillet and cook for 15 to 20 minutes, until golden on both sides. Remove chicken to a plate; cover with aluminum foil and set aside. Add onion, green pepper and garlic to drippings in skillet; cook and stir until vegetables are tender. Add broth, scraping up brown bits in bottom of skillet. Add remaining ingredients; stir until blended. Return chicken to skillet, spooning some of the sauce over chicken. Cover and cook for about one hour, until chicken is tender and juices run clear.

Nutrition Per Serving: *395 calories, 12g total fat, 1g sat fat, 160mg cholesterol, 720mg sodium, 16g carbohydrate, 3g fiber, 54g protein*

Chicken Cacciatore

Creamy Chicken & Biscuits

Creamy Chicken & Biscuits

Serves 8.

2 c. new redskin potatoes, halved or quartered
2 c. carrots, peeled and sliced
1 onion, diced
3 T. butter
3 T. all-purpose flour
salt and pepper to taste
2 c. milk
1 c. low-sodium chicken broth
2 cubes low-sodium chicken bouillon
2 boneless, skinless chicken breasts, cooked and diced
12-oz. tube large refrigerated biscuits, cut into quarters

Cover potatoes, carrots and onion with water in a medium saucepan. Bring to a boil over medium heat; reduce heat and simmer until tender. Drain and set aside. Melt butter in another medium saucepan; stir in flour, salt and pepper, stirring constantly. Gradually add milk, broth and bouillon. Cook until thickened, about 3 to 5 minutes; set aside. Combine chicken and vegetables in a lightly greased 13"x9" baking pan. Pour sauce over top; arrange biscuits over sauce. Bake, uncovered, at 400 degrees for 15 minutes, or until biscuits are golden and sauce is bubbly.

Nutrition Per Serving: 290 calories, 12g total fat, 5g sat fat, 34mg cholesterol, 532mg sodium, 31g carbohydrate, 2g fiber, 13g protein

Quick tip

Salsa in a jiffy! Pour a can of stewed tomatoes, several slices of canned jalapeño pepper and a teaspoon or two of the jalapeño juice into a blender. Cover and process mixture to the desired consistency.

Salmon Patties

Makes 4 servings.

14-3/4 oz. can salmon, drained and 2 T. liquid reserved
1 egg, beaten
1/3 c. onion, minced
1/4 c. all-purpose flour
2 t. baking powder
2 T. canola oil
salt and pepper to taste

Combine salmon, egg, onion and flour in a medium bowl; set aside. In a small bowl, mix together reserved salmon liquid and baking powder; stir into salmon mixture. Form into 4 patties. Heat oil in a large skillet over medium heat; add patties. Cook until golden on both sides. Sprinkle with salt and pepper.

Nutrition Per Serving: 264 calories, 17g total fat, 3g sat fat, 125mg cholesterol, 735mg sodium, 6g carbohydrate, 0g fiber, 24g protein

Salmon Patties

Barbecued Pork Chops
Makes 8 servings.

8 pork chops
3 T. oil
1/2 c. catsup
1/3 c. vinegar
1 c. water
1 t. celery seed
1/2 t. nutmeg
1 bay leaf

In a large skillet over medium heat, brown chops in oil. Drain; arrange chops in a greased 13"x9" baking pan. Combine remaining ingredients and pour over chops. Cover with aluminum foil. Bake at 325 degrees for 1-1/2 hours, until tender. Discard bay leaf before serving. Add salt and pepper to taste.

Nutrition Per Serving: 334 calories, 17g total fat, 5g sat fat, 106mg cholesterol, 253mg sodium, 5g carbohydrate, 0g fiber, 38g protein

Barbecued Pork Chops

Black Bean & Rice Enchiladas
Makes 8 servings.

1 green pepper, chopped
1/4 c. onion, chopped
3 cloves garlic, minced
1 T. olive oil
15-oz. can black beans, drained and rinsed
14-1/4 oz. can diced tomatoes with green chiles
1/4 c. taco sauce
1 T. chili powder
1 t. ground cumin
1/4 t. red pepper flakes
2 c. cooked brown rice
8 10-inch multi-grain flour tortillas
1 c. salsa
1/2 c. shredded low-fat Cheddar cheese
3 T. fresh cilantro, chopped

In a skillet over medium heat, sauté green pepper, onion and garlic in oil until tender. Add beans, tomatoes, taco sauce and seasonings. Simmer until heated through and mixture thickens. Add rice; cook 5 minutes. Spoon filling down the center of each tortilla. Roll up tortillas; place in a lightly greased 13"x9" baking pan. Spoon salsa over tortillas. Bake, covered, at 350 degrees for 25 minutes. Uncover; sprinkle with cheese and cilantro. Bake an additional 3 minutes, until cheese is melted.

Nutrition Per Serving: 262 calories, 4g total fat, 1g sat fat, 5mg cholesterol, 766mg sodium, 48g carbohydrate, 10g fiber, 14g protein

Black Bean & Rice Enchiladas

Balsamic Chicken & Pears

Balsamic Chicken & Pears

Serves 4.

3 t. oil, divided
4 boneless, skinless chicken breasts
2 Bosc pears, cored and cut into 8 wedges
1 c. low-sodium chicken broth
3 T. balsamic vinegar
2 t. cornstarch
1-1/2 t. sugar
1/4 c. dried cherries or raisins

Heat 2 teaspoons oil in a large non-stick skillet over medium-high heat; add chicken. Cook until golden and cooked through, about 4 to 5 minutes per side. Transfer to a plate; keep warm. Heat remaining oil in same skillet; add pears and cook until tender and golden. In a small bowl, combine remaining ingredients except cherries or raisins. Stir broth mixture into skillet with pears; add cherries or raisins. Bring to a boil over medium heat. Cook for one minute, stirring constantly. Return chicken to pan; heat through. Serve pear sauce over chicken.

Nutrition Per Serving: *267 calories, 5g total fat, 0g sat fat, 80mg cholesterol, 92mg sodium, 28g carbohydrate, 3g fiber, 27g protein*

Quick tip

Freezing extra pieces of chicken? Add a flavorful marinade to plastic zipping bags of uncooked chicken and freeze. When you thaw it for cooking, the chicken will be deliciously seasoned. So convenient!

Rosemary Roast Pork Loin

Makes 8 servings.

3-lb. boneless pork loin roast
2 t. dried rosemary
2 t. dry mustard
1 t. ground ginger
1 t. salt
1 t. pepper
2 T. olive oil
4 cloves garlic, minced

Place roast in an ungreased shallow roasting pan; set aside. Crush together seasonings in a mortar and pestle. Add oil and garlic to make a paste. Spread mixture over roast; let stand at room temperature for 30 to 45 minutes. Bake, uncovered, at 350 degrees for one to 1-1/2 hours. Let stand 15 to 20 minutes before slicing.

Nutrition Per Serving: *310 calories, 17g total fat, 6g sat fat, 114mg cholesterol, 386mg sodium, 1g carbohydrate, 0g fiber, 37g protein*

Rosemary Roast Pork Loin

Barbara's Open-House Waffles

Serves 8.

3 c. biscuit baking mix
1 c. millet flour
1/8 t. baking soda
1/4 c. canola oil
3 eggs, beaten
3 c. buttermilk
2 T. water
Garnish: maple syrup, fresh strawberries, plain yogurt

In a bowl, whisk together baking mix, flour and baking soda. Add remaining ingredients except garnish and mix well. Drop batter by 1/2 cupfuls onto a heated waffle iron; cook according to manufacturer's directions. Garnish as desired.

Nutrition Per Serving: *377 calories, 17g total fat, 3g sat fat, 84mg cholesterol, 700mg sodium, 44g carbohydrate, 1g fiber, 10g protein*

Barbara's Open-House Waffles

Apple-Stuffed French Toast

Makes 4 servings.

3 apples, peeled, cored and cut into chunks
2 T. brown sugar, packed
cinnamon to taste
2 eggs, beaten
1/2 c. 2% milk
1 t. vanilla extract
8 slices wheat bread
2 t. powdered sugar

In a microwave-safe bowl, combine apples, brown sugar and cinnamon. Cover and microwave on high for 5 minutes, until apples are soft. In a separate bowl, stir together eggs, milk and vanilla. Spray a griddle or large frying pan with non-stick vegetable spray and heat over medium heat. Quickly dip the bread on both sides in the egg mixture and place on the griddle. Cook until golden on both sides. Place one slice of toast on a plate; put a scoop of the apple mixture in the middle. Top with another slice of toast. Dust with powdered sugar.

Nutrition Per Serving: *326 calories, 6g total fat, 1g sat fat, 110mg cholesterol, 429mg sodium, 60g carbohydrate, 9g fiber, 12g protein*

Quick tip

If you love fresh cranberries, stock up when they're available and pop unopened bags in the freezer. You'll be able to add their fruity tang to recipes year 'round.

Apple-Stuffed French Toast

Yummy Blueberry Waffles

Makes 4 waffles. Serves 4.

2 eggs
2 c. all-purpose flour
1-3/4 c. milk
1/2 c. oil
1 T. sugar
4 t. baking powder
1/4 t. salt
1/2 t. vanilla extract
1-1/2 c. blueberries

In a large bowl, beat eggs with an electric mixer on medium speed until fluffy. Add remaining ingredients except berries; beat just until smooth. Spray a waffle iron with non-stick vegetable spray. Pour batter by 1/2 cupfuls onto the preheated waffle iron. Scatter berries over batter. Bake according to manufacturer's directions, until golden.

Nutrition Per Serving: 552 calories, 31g total fat, 5g sat fat, 112mg cholesterol, 715mg sodium, 58g carbohydrate, 1g fiber, 13g protein

Mom's Lasagna

Makes 10 servings.

15-oz. container low-fat ricotta cheese
1 egg, beaten
10-oz. pkg. frozen chopped spinach, thawed and well drained
9 lasagna noodles, cooked
1/2 c. grated Parmesan cheese
1 c. low-fat shredded mozzarella cheese
4 slices mozzarella cheese

Prepare Sauce; set aside. Combine ricotta, egg and spinach. Spoon a thin layer of sauce into an ungreased 13"x9" baking pan. Cover with a layer of lasagna noodles, sauce, ricotta mixture, Parmesan and shredded mozzarella. Repeat layers 2 more times, ending with sauce; top with sliced mozzarella. Cover with aluminum foil; bake at 350 degrees for 45 minutes. Uncover; continue to bake until golden on top. Let stand 15 minutes before slicing.

Sauce:

1/2 c. onion, minced
1 clove garlic, pressed
1 T. olive oil
1 lb. ground Italian turkey sausage
2 14-1/2 oz. cans Italian stewed tomatoes, diced
8-oz. can no-salt tomato sauce
6-oz. can tomato paste
1/2 c. no-salt tomato juice
2 T. low-sodium Worcestershire sauce
1 t. sugar
1 t. dried basil
1 t. dried oregano
2 drops hot pepper sauce

In a Dutch oven over medium heat, sauté onion and garlic in oil until tender. Add sausage and brown, about 10 minutes. Drain. Stir in remaining ingredients. Cover; simmer over low heat for one hour.

Nutrition Per Serving: 348 calories, 15g total fat, 7g sat fat, 91mg cholesterol, 843mg sodium, 25g carbohydrate, 4g fiber, 25g protein

Mom's Lasagna

Sandwiches, Burgers & Pizzas

(favorite fork-free recipes)

Can "comfort food" and "lightened up" be in the same recipe?
Of course they can! Get off to a fresh and healthier start with
some of your favorite satisfying sandwiches, burgers and pizzas
that are lightened up and still yummy! Sink your teeth into
an arugula and turkey All-American Sandwich, enjoy a juicy
Gobblin' Good Turkey Burger or grab a slice of a wheat-crust
Basil Mushroom Pizza. Go ahead, get comfortable with your
tasty, healthier lifestyle.

Sandwiches, Burgers & Pizzas

Mom's Chili Dogs

Mom's Chili Dogs

Makes 12 servings.

1 lb. lean ground beef
1 onion, chopped
1/2 c. catsup
6-oz. can no-salt tomato paste
2-1/4 c. water
3 T. chili powder
1 t. salt
12 reduced-fat hot dogs, cooked
12 hot dog buns

Brown ground beef until no longer pink. Combine all ingredients except hot dogs and buns in a large stockpot over medium-high heat; stir well. Cover; bring to a boil.

Reduce heat to low; simmer for one to 2 hours, stirring occasionally to break up beef. To serve, spoon over hot dogs in buns.

Nutrition Per Serving: *291 calories, 11g total fat, 4g sat fat, 54mg cholesterol, 934mg sodium, 28g carbohydrate, 1g fiber, 16g protein*

Basil Mushroom Pizza

Makes 6 servings.

1 T. butter
1 c. portabella mushrooms, sliced
2 cloves garlic, minced
12-inch whole-grain Italian pizza crust
1 T. olive oil
1 c. fresh spinach, sliced into 1/2-inch strips
1/2 c. fresh basil, chopped
8-oz. pkg. shredded low-fat mozzarella cheese

Melt butter in a large skillet over medium heat. Add mushrooms and garlic; sauté just until tender, about 5 minutes. Place crust on an ungreased baking sheet; brush with oil. Sprinkle spinach evenly over crust, followed by basil, mushroom mixture and cheese. Bake at 350 degrees for 8 to 10 minutes, or until cheese is melted and edges of crust are crisp.

Nutrition Per Serving: *315 calories, 12g total fat, 5g sat fat, 25mg cholesterol, 635mg sodium, 34g carbohydrate, 1g fiber, 17g protein*

Basil Mushroom Pizza

Steak & Egg Breakfast Burrito

Makes 2 servings.

2 frozen sliced beef sandwich steaks
4 eggs
2 T. milk
2 t. fresh chives, chopped
salt and pepper to taste
2 corn tortillas
salsa to taste
1/2 c. shredded low-fat Mexican-blend cheese, divided

In a skillet over medium heat, cook steaks until no longer pink; drain and set aside. Beat together eggs, milk, chives, salt and pepper. In same skillet, scramble eggs to desired doneness. Divide eggs evenly between tortillas; top each with steak, salsa and cheese. Roll up and microwave on high setting for 20 to 30 seconds to melt cheese.

Nutrition Per Serving: *389 calories, 24g total fat, 9g sat fat, 463mg cholesterol, 383mg sodium, 15g carbohydrate, 2g fiber, 27g protein*

Steak & Egg Breakfast Burrito

Nacho Burgers

Serves 5.

1 small avocado, pitted, peeled and diced
1 plum tomato, diced
2 green onions, chopped
2 t. lime juice
1-1/4 lbs. lean ground beef
1 egg, beaten
3/4 c. nacho-flavored tortilla chips, crushed
1/4 c. fresh cilantro, chopped
1/2 t. chili powder
1/2 t. ground cumin
salt and pepper to taste
1-1/4 c. low-fat shredded Pepper Jack cheese
5 wheat hamburger buns, split

Mix together avocado, tomato, onions and lime juice; mash slightly and set aside. Combine beef, egg, chips and seasonings in a large bowl. Form into 5 patties; grill to desired doneness, turning to cook on both sides. Sprinkle cheese over burgers; grill until melted. Serve on buns; spread with avocado mixture.

Nutrition Per Serving: *524 calories, 30g total fat, 11g sat fat, 140mg cholesterol, 448mg sodium, 27g carbohydrate, 6g fiber, 38g protein*

Nacho Burgers

Lynda's Salmon Burgers

Lynda's Salmon Burgers

Makes 8 servings.

1 lb. salmon fillet, skin removed and chopped
1/2 c. red onion, finely chopped
1/4 c. fresh basil, thinly sliced
1/4 t. salt
1/4 t. pepper
1 egg white
1 T. sriracha hot chili sauce
Optional: 1/4 c. panko bread crumbs
8 slices whole-grain bread, toasted and cut in half
Garnish: lettuce and tomato

In a large bowl, combine salmon, onion, basil and seasonings; mix gently. In a small bowl, whisk together egg white and chili sauce. Add to salmon mixture and stir well to combine. If mixture is too soft, stir in bread crumbs. Form mixture into 4 patties, 1/2-inch thick. Heat a large non-stick skillet over medium-high heat. Coat pan with non-stick vegetable spray. Add patties to skillet; cook for about 3 minutes per side. Place patties sandwich-style on toasted wheat bread and garnish with lettuce and tomato.

Nutrition Per Serving: *196 calories, 9g total fat, 2g sat fat, 31mg cholesterol, 311mg sodium, 14g carbohydrate, 2g fiber, 16g protein*

Toasted Chicken Salad Bagels

Makes 12 servings.

6 c. cooked chicken, chopped
2 c. celery, chopped
1 c. almonds, chopped and toasted
1/4 c. lemon juice
1/4 c. onion, grated
1 c. low-fat mayonnaise
1 c. shredded low-fat Cheddar cheese
12 whole-grain bagels, sliced
1 c. baked potato chips, crushed

In a bowl, combine all ingredients except bagels and chips. Spread mixture on bottom halves of bagels. Transfer bagels and tops to an ungreased baking sheet. Broil for 3 to 5 minutes, until golden. Sprinkle chips on chicken mixture. Replace bagel tops.

Nutrition Per Serving: *478 calories, 13g total fat, 2g sat fat, 61mg cholesterol, 956mg sodium, 54g carbohydrate, 9g fiber, 37g protein*

Quick tip

Garden-fresh herbs are delicious. If you have them on hand, just use double the amount of dried herbs called for in a recipe.

Sandwiches, Burgers & Pizzas

Tuna Panini
Serves 4.

12-oz. can tuna, drained
1 small onion, chopped
2 low-salt dill pickle spears, chopped
3/4 c. carrot, peeled, shredded and chopped
3/4 c. shredded low-fat mozzarella cheese
2 T. low-fat mayonnaise
1 T. olive oil
8 slices multi-grain bread, toasted
1 tomato, sliced

In a bowl, mix tuna, onion, pickles, carrot, cheese and mayonnaise. In a panini press or skillet, heat olive oil over medium heat until hot. For each sandwich, top one slice of toasted bread with tuna mixture, 2 slices of tomato and second slice of bread. Place sandwich in a panini press or skillet; heat one to 2 minutes, or until cheese is melted.

Nutrition Per Serving: *352 calories, 10g total fat, 3g sat fat, 37mg cholesterol, 659mg sodium, 30g carbohydrate, 5g fiber, 36g protein*

The Ultimate Shrimp Sandwich
Serves 6.

3/4 lb. cooked shrimp, chopped
1/4 c. green pepper, chopped
1/4 c. celery, chopped
1/4 c. cucumber, chopped
1/4 c. tomato, diced
1/4 c. green onion, chopped
1/4 c. low-fat mayonnaise
Optional: hot pepper sauce to taste
6 split-top wheat rolls, split and lightly toasted
1 c. lettuce, shredded

In a bowl, combine shrimp, vegetables and mayonnaise; toss well. Set aside. Divide lettuce among rolls. Top with shrimp mixture.

Nutrition Per Serving: *223 calories, 8g total fat, 3g sat fat, 96mg cholesterol, 382mg sodium, 24g carbohydrate, 4g fiber, 16g protein*

Tuna Panini

Quick tip
Only using part of an onion? The remaining half will stay fresh for days when rubbed with butter or oil and stored in the refrigerator.

The Ultimate Shrimp Sandwich

Chicken Pitas

Chicken Pitas

Makes 4 servings.

1/2 c. plain yogurt
1/4 c. cucumber, finely chopped
1/2 t. dill weed
1/4 t. dried mint, crushed
4 pita bread rounds
4 lettuce leaves
2 c. cooked chicken, cubed
1 tomato, thinly sliced
1/3 c. crumbled feta cheese

In a small bowl, stir together yogurt, cucumber, dill weed and mint; set aside. For each sandwich, layer a pita with lettuce, chicken, tomato and cheese. Spoon yogurt mixture on top. Roll up pita and secure with a wooden toothpick. Serve immediately.

Nutrition Per Serving: *252 calories, 6g total fat, 3g sat fat, 72mg cholesterol, 364mg sodium, 20g carbohydrate, 1g fiber, 28g protein*

Gobblin' Good Turkey Burgers

Serves 6.

1 lb. ground turkey
1 onion, minced
1/2 c. shredded low-fat Cheddar cheese
1/4 c. low-sodium Worcestershire sauce
1/2 t. dry mustard
salt and pepper to taste
6 whole-grain hamburger buns, split
Garnish: lettuce, tomato

Combine all ingredients except buns; form into 6 patties. Grill until well-done; serve on hamburger buns. Garnish as desired.

Nutrition Per Serving: *246 calories, 8g total fat, 2g sat fat, 62mg cholesterol, 389mg sodium, 23g carbohydrate, 3g fiber, 22g protein*

Gobblin' Good
Turkey Burgers

Key West Burgers

Serves 4.

1 lb. lean ground beef
3 T. Key lime juice
1/4 c. fresh cilantro, chopped
salt and pepper to taste
4 wheat hamburger buns, split and toasted
Garnish: lettuce

In a bowl, combine beef, lime juice, cilantro, salt and pepper. Form beef mixture into 4 patties. Spray a large skillet with non-stick vegetable spray. Cook patties over medium heat for 6 minutes. Flip patties, cover skillet and cook for another 6 minutes. Place lettuce on bottom halves of buns and top with patties. Add Creamy Burger Spread onto bun tops and close sandwiches.

Creamy Burger Spread:

1/2 c. light cream cheese, softened
1/2 c. plain Greek yogurt
3 green onion tops, chopped

Combine all ingredients until completely blended. Cover and refrigerate at least 15 minutes.

Nutrition Per Serving: 204 calories, 7g total fat, 3g sat fat, 21mg cholesterol, 30mg sodium, 24g carbohydrate, 3g fiber, 13g protein

Egg Salad Minis

Serves 7.

4 eggs, hard-boiled, peeled and chopped
1/4 c. onion, finely chopped
1/4 c. low-fat mayonnaise
salt and pepper to taste
14 slices soft sandwich wheat bread, crusts removed

Using a fork, mash eggs. Stir in onion. Add mayonnaise and seasoning to taste. Spoon egg mixture onto 7 bread slices. Top with remaining bread and cut diagonally in quarters. Makes 28 mini sandwiches.

Nutrition Per Serving: 146 calories, 5g total fat, 1g sat fat, 121mg cholesterol, 300mg sodium, 18g carbohydrate, 1g fiber, 8g protein

Zucchini-Crust Pizza

Makes 6 servings.

2 c. zucchini, shredded and packed
2 eggs, beaten
1/3 c. whole-wheat flour
1/2 c. shredded mozzarella cheese
1/2 c. shredded low-fat pizza-blend cheese
1 T. olive oil
1 T. fresh basil, chopped
Garnish: favorite pizza toppings such as tomatoes, basil
    and fresh mozzarella cheese

In a strainer, press zucchini to remove as much liquid as possible. Combine zucchini and remaining ingredients except garnish in a bowl; stir well. Spread mixture in a parchment paper-lined 12" round pizza pan. Smooth out mixture to cover pan. Bake at 375 degrees for 35 minutes, or until set. Top with desired toppings; return to oven until heated through. Cut into wedges to serve.

Nutrition Per Serving: 124 calories, 7g total fat, 3g sat fat, 81mg cholesterol, 148mg sodium, 7g carbohydrate, 1g fiber, 9g protein

Zucchini-Crust Pizza

Veggie Melts

Easy Beef Boats

Makes 6 servings.

2 lbs. lean ground beef
1/2 c. onion, chopped
1/2 t. garlic powder
1/2 t. salt
1/2 t. pepper
1 loaf French bread, halved lengthwise
1 c. plain low-fat Greek yogurt
2 tomatoes, diced
1 green pepper, diced
1/2 c. shredded low-fat Cheddar cheese

In a skillet over medium heat, brown beef and onion. Drain; stir in seasonings. Open up bread and place on an ungreased baking sheet. Remove skillet from heat; stir in Greek yogurt. Spoon beef mixture onto bread; sprinkle with remaining ingredients. Bake at 350 degrees for 20 minutes, or until cheese is melted. If crisper bread is desired, bake a little longer. Slice into 3-inch portions to serve.

Nutrition Per Serving: *500 calories, 17g total fat, 7g sat fat, 99mg cholesterol, 785mg sodium, 41g carbohydrate, 2g fiber, 44g protein*

Veggie Melts

Makes 4 servings.

1 c. sliced baby portabella mushrooms
1/4 c. olive oil
1 loaf ciabatta bread, halved horizontally
8-oz. jar whole roasted red peppers, drained
1-1/2 t. Italian seasoning
1 c. shredded Fontina cheese

In a skillet over medium heat, sauté mushrooms in olive oil until tender. Place bread halves on an ungreased baking sheet. On one bread half, layer peppers, mushrooms and Italian seasoning. Top both halves evenly with cheese. Broil until lightly golden. Assemble sandwich and cut into 4 pieces.

Nutrition Per Serving: *470 calories, 22g total fat, 7g sat fat, 31mg cholesterol, 938mg sodium, 52g carbohydrate, 2g fiber, 15g protein*

Easy Beef Boats

Raspberry-Dijon Chicken Baguettes

Serves 4.

4 boneless, skinless chicken breasts
4 mini baguette rolls, halved lengthwise
8 t. Dijon mustard
8 t. no-sugar-added raspberry spread
1-1/2 c. fresh arugula, torn
4 thin slices red onion

Broil or grill chicken until golden and juices run clear; slice. Spread bottom half of baguettes with mustard; spread top half with raspberry spread. Layer grilled chicken over mustard; top with arugula and onion. Add top half of baguettes.

Nutrition Per Serving: 337 calories, 3g total fat, 1g sat fat, 68mg cholesterol, 735mg sodium, 41g carbohydrate, 4g fiber, 35g protein

Mom's Eggplant Sandwich

Serves 6.

1 eggplant, peeled and sliced 1/2-inch thick
2 zucchini or yellow squash, sliced 1/2-inch thick
salt and pepper to taste
2 T. olive oil
1/4 c. low-fat mayonnaise
1 French baguette loaf, halved lengthwise
1 tomato, thinly sliced
1/4 c. grated Parmesan cheese, divided

Sprinkle eggplant and squash slices with salt and pepper; set aside. Heat oil in a grill pan over medium heat. Grill eggplant and squash until veggies are tender and have grill marks; drain on a paper towel. Spread mayonnaise over cut sides of loaf. Arrange tomato slices on bottom half; sprinkle with salt, pepper and half of Parmesan cheese. Layer grilled eggplant and squash over tomatoes. Sprinkle with remaining cheese and add top half; slice into 6 pieces.

Nutrition Per Serving: 242 calories, 5g total fat, 1g sat fat, 4mg cholesterol, 524mg sodium, 39g carbohydrate, 5g fiber, 10g protein

Bestest Burger Ever

Serves 8.

2 lbs. lean ground beef
1 onion, chopped
1 t. salt
1 t. pepper
1 t. dried basil
1/3 c. low-sodium teriyaki sauce
1/4 c. Italian-seasoned dry bread crumbs
1 T. grated Parmesan cheese
4 slices light American cheese, halved
8 sesame wheat rolls, split
Garnish: fresh arugula, sliced cucumber

Mix together beef, onion, salt, pepper and basil. Add teriyaki sauce, bread crumbs and Parmesan cheese; mix well. Divide into 8 patties. Grill to desired doneness; top with American cheese. Serve on sesame rolls with arugula and sliced cucumber.

Nutrition Per Serving: 356 calories, 14g total fat, 5g sat fat, 77mg cholesterol, 943mg sodium, 25g carbohydrate, 3g fiber, 32g protein

Bestest Burger Ever

Chicken Tacos

Serves 8.

2 T. olive oil
1 onion, chopped
2 T. garlic, minced
2 lbs. boneless, skinless chicken thighs or breasts, cut into bite-size pieces
10-oz. can diced tomatoes with green chiles
4-oz. can diced green chiles
1/8 t. hot pepper sauce
1 T. dried cilantro
salt and pepper to taste
12-oz. pkg. 6-inch corn tortillas
Garnish: shredded low-fat Cheddar cheese

Heat oil in a large skillet over medium heat. Sauté onion and garlic until tender. Add chicken and cook through. Stir in remaining ingredients except tortillas and cheese; reduce heat. Stirring often, simmer 8 to 10 minutes, until most of the liquid is cooked out. Spoon into tortillas and garnish with cheese.

Nutrition Per Serving: *346 calories, 10g total fat, 2g sat fat, 109mg cholesterol, 301mg sodium, 21g carbohydrate, 3g fiber, 42g protein*

Chicken Tacos

BBQ Chicken Pizza

Serves 4.

12-inch Italian pizza crust
3 c. cooked chicken, shredded
1 c. low-sodium barbecue sauce
1/2 c. shredded low-sodium mozzarella cheese
1/2 c. shredded low-sodium Cheddar cheese

Place pizza crust on a lightly greased 12" round pizza pan. Combine chicken and barbecue sauce; spread on pizza crust. Sprinkle with cheeses. Bake at 450 degrees for 8 to 10 minutes, or until cheeses melt and crust is crisp.

Nutrition Per Serving: *565 calories, 14g total fat, 5g sat fat, 81mg cholesterol, 801mg sodium, 65g carbohydrate, 1g fiber, 39g protein*

Quick tip

Serve that favorite burger or pizza with a fresh and healthy green salad. Give the salad a fresh new taste. Instead of using white vinegar to make salad dressing, add a splash of fruit-flavored vinegar.

BBQ Chicken Pizza

Chicken Quesadillas El Grande

Chicken Quesadillas El Grande

Serves 8.

1 lb. sliced reduced-sodium roast deli chicken, shredded
3 T. salsa
salt and pepper to taste
1 small onion, cut into strips
1 green pepper, cut into strips
3 T. olive oil
15-oz. can reduced-sodium refried beans
8 10-inch flour tortillas
6-oz. pkg. shredded low-fat Mexican-blend cheese
Garnish: shredded lettuce, diced tomatoes,
    Greek yogurt, diced onion, additional salsa

In a bowl, stir together chicken, salsa, salt and pepper; set aside. In a skillet over medium heat, cook onion and pepper in oil until crisp-tender; remove to a bowl. Evenly spread refried beans onto 4 tortillas. For each quesadilla, place one tortilla, bean-side up, in a skillet coated with non-stick vegetable spray. Top with a quarter of chicken, onion mixture and cheese. Place a plain tortilla on top. Cook over medium heat until layers start to warm, about 2 minutes. Flip over and cook until tortilla is crisp and filling is hot. Cut each quesadilla into wedges and garnish as desired.

Nutrition Per Serving: *349 calories, 13g total fat, 2g sat fat, 39mg cholesterol, 909mg sodium, 37g carbohydrate, 6g fiber, 23g protein*

All-American Sandwiches

Serves 4.

1-1/2 T. olive oil
1 red onion, thinly sliced
3-1/2 T. red wine vinegar
6 c. fresh arugula leaves, divided
1/4 c. low-fat mayonnaise
salt and pepper to taste
4 whole-grain ciabatta rolls, halved
3/4 lb. thinly sliced reduced-sodium smoked deli turkey
1/4 c. crumbled blue cheese

Heat oil in a skillet over medium-high heat. Add onion and sauté until soft and lightly golden. Remove from heat and stir in vinegar. Set aside. Chop enough arugula to equal one cup. Stir in mayonnaise; season with salt and pepper. Spread arugula mixture over cut sides of rolls. Divide turkey evenly among bottom halves of rolls. Top with cheese, onion mixture, remaining arugula leaves and top halves of rolls.

Nutrition Per Serving: *379 calories, 11g total fat, 2g sat fat, 57mg cholesterol, 1063mg sodium, 42g carbohydrate, 3g fiber, 27g protein*

All-American Sandwiches

Deep-Dish Sausage Pizza

Makes 8 servings.

16-oz. pkg. frozen bread dough, thawed
1/2 lb. sweet Italian pork sausage, casings removed
1-1/2 c. shredded low-fat mozzarella cheese
1 green pepper, diced
1 red pepper, diced
28-oz. can diced tomatoes, drained
3/4 t. dried oregano
1/2 t. salt
1/4 t. garlic powder
1/2 c. grated Parmesan cheese

Press dough into the bottom and up the sides of a greased 13"x9" baking pan; set aside. In a large skillet, crumble sausage and cook until no longer pink; drain. Sprinkle sausage over dough; top with mozzarella cheese. In the same skillet, sauté peppers until slightly tender. Stir in tomatoes and seasonings; spoon over pizza. Sprinkle with Parmesan cheese. Bake, uncovered, at 350 degrees for 25 to 35 minutes, until crust is golden.

Nutrition Per Serving: 332 calories, 15g total fat, 6g sat fat, 40mg cholesterol, 978mg sodium, 32g carbohydrate, 2g fiber, 18g protein

Deep-Dish Sausage Pizza

Aloha Burgers

Serves 4.

8-oz. can pineapple slices, drained and juice reserved
3/4 c. low-sodium teriyaki sauce
1 lb. ground turkey
1 T. butter, softened
4 wheat sandwich thins, split
2 slices Swiss cheese, halved
4 slices reduced-sodium bacon, crisply cooked
4 leaves lettuce
1 red onion, sliced

Stir together reserved pineapple juice and teriyaki sauce in a small bowl. Place pineapple slices and 3 tablespoons juice mixture into a plastic zipping bag. Turn to coat; set aside. Shape ground beef into 4 patties and spoon remaining juice mixture over top; set aside. Spread butter on buns; set aside. Grill patties over medium-high heat until well done, turning to cook on both sides. Place buns on grill, cut-side down, to toast lightly. Remove pineapple slices from plastic bag; place on grill and heat through until lightly golden, about one minute per side. Serve burgers on buns topped with pineapple, cheese, bacon, lettuce and onion.

Nutrition Per Serving: 419 calories, 20g total fat, 8g sat fat, 111mg cholesterol, 480mg sodium, 32g carbohydrate, 7g fiber, 31g protein

Aloha Burgers

Grilled Cheese Sandwich

Grilled Cheese Sandwich

Serves 2.

3 slices whole-grain sprouted bread
2 slices Havarti cheese
2 slices low-fat Cheddar cheese
2 slices tomato
6 slices cucumber
1 T. canola oil
1 T. butter

On one slice of bread, layer one piece of each cheese, one slice tomato and 3 cucumber slices. Place another piece of bread on top. Layer remaining cheeses, tomato and cucumber. Add third slice of bread on top. In a small skillet, heat oil and butter. Lay sandwich in pan and heat for one minute. Turn over and heat other side until golden. Turn again and place aluminum foil on top until both sides are golden and cheese melts. Cut sandwich in half.

Nutrition Per Serving: *352 calories, 22g total fat, 10g sat fat, 41mg cholesterol, 502mg sodium, 20g carbohydrate, 3g fiber, 17g protein*

Greek Pita Pizza

Makes 8 servings.

10-oz. pkg. frozen chopped spinach, thawed and well drained
4 green onions, chopped
1 T. fresh dill, chopped
garlic salt and pepper to taste
4 whole-wheat pita rounds, split
4 roma tomatoes, sliced 1/2-inch thick
1/2 c. crumbled feta cheese with basil & tomato
dried oregano or Greek seasoning to taste

Mix spinach, onions and dill in a small bowl. Season with garlic salt and pepper; set aside. Place pita rounds on ungreased baking sheets. Arrange tomato slices among pitas. Spread spinach mixture evenly over tomatoes; spread cheese over tomatoes. Sprinkle with desired seasoning. Bake at 450 degrees for 10 to 15 minutes, until crisp. Cut into wedges.

Nutrition Per Serving: *254 calories, 6g total fat, 3g sat fat, 17mg cholesterol, 606mg sodium, 42g carbohydrate, 8g fiber, 12g protein*

Greek Pita Pizza

Mom's Homemade Pizza

Mom's Homemade Pizza

Makes 8 servings.

8-oz. can tomato sauce
1/2 t. sugar
1/4 t. pepper
1 t. garlic powder
1-1/2 t. dried thyme
3 T. grated Parmesan cheese
1 onion, finely chopped
5 Roma tomatoes, sliced
1 c. fresh spinach, chopped
1 c. shredded low-fat mozzarella cheese

Prepare Pizza Dough. Combine tomato sauce, sugar and seasonings; spread over dough. Top with Parmesan cheese, onion, tomatoes, spinach and shredded cheese. Bake at 400 degrees for 25 to 30 minutes, until edges are golden.

Pizza Dough:

1 env. quick-rise yeast
1 c. hot water
2 T. olive oil
1/2 t. salt
3 c. all-purpose flour, divided
1 T. cornmeal

Combine yeast and water. Let stand 5 minutes. Add olive oil, salt and half of the flour. Stir to combine. Stir in remaining flour. Gather into a ball and place in oiled bowl. Turn dough over and cover with plastic wrap. Let rise 30 minutes. Brush oil over a 15"x10" jelly-roll pan or 2, 12" round pizza pans; sprinkle with cornmeal. Roll out dough; place on pan.

Nutrition Per Serving: 193 calories, 6g total fat, 2g sat fat, 6mg cholesterol, 327mg sodium, 28g carbohydrate, 2g fiber, 7g protein

Grilled Chicken & Zucchini Wraps

Grilled Chicken & Zucchini Wraps

Makes 8 servings.

4 boneless, skinless chicken breasts
6 zucchini, sliced lengthwise into 1/4-inch thick slices
2 T. olive oil
salt and pepper to taste
1/4 c. low-fat ranch salad dressing, divided
8 10-inch whole-grain flour tortillas
8 leaves lettuce
1/4 c. shredded low-fat Cheddar cheese

Brush chicken and zucchini with olive oil; sprinkle with salt and pepper. Grill chicken over medium-high heat for 5 minutes. Turn chicken over; add zucchini to grill. Grill 5 minutes longer, or until chicken juices run clear and zucchini is tender. Slice chicken into strips; set aside. For each wrap, spread salad dressing on a tortilla. Top with a lettuce leaf, chicken and zucchini. Sprinkle with cheese; roll up.

Nutrition Per Serving: 297 calories, 10g total fat, 1g sat fat, 21mg cholesterol, 501mg sodium, 38g carbohydrate, 7g fiber, 16g protein

Family Favorite Pork Tacos

Family Favorite Pork Tacos

Serves 8.

2 t. oil
1-lb. pork tenderloin, cubed
1 t. ground cumin
2 cloves garlic, minced
1 c. green or red salsa
Optional: 1/2 c. fresh cilantro, chopped
8 10-inch corn tortillas, warmed
Garnish: shredded lettuce, diced tomatoes, sliced
  avocado, sliced black olives, plain yogurt, shredded
  low-fat Cheddar cheese

Heat oil in a skillet over medium-high heat. Add pork
and cumin; cook until golden on all sides and pork is
no longer pink in the center, about 8 to 10 minutes. Add
garlic and cook for one minute; drain. Stir in salsa and

heat through; stir in cilantro, if using. Using 2 forks,
shred pork. Fill warmed tortillas with pork mixture;
garnish as desired.

*Nutrition Per Serving: 193 calories, 6g total fat, 1g sat fat,
53mg cholesterol, 236mg sodium, 14g carbohydrate, 3g fiber,
19g protein*

Vegetable Quesadillas

Serves 6.

8-oz. pkg. low-fat shredded Cheddar or Monterey
  Jack cheese
1/4 c. onion, grated
15-oz. can corn, drained
15-oz. can black beans, drained and rinsed
8-oz. jar salsa
6 10-inch flour tortillas

In a bowl, combine all ingredients except tortillas; mix
well. Evenly spoon mixture onto one half of each tortilla;
fold over and gently press together. Working in batches,
place tortillas in a lightly greased skillet over medium
heat. Cook until golden; flip and cook until other side is
golden. Slice into wedges to serve.

*Nutrition Per Serving: 297 calories, 8g total fat, 2g sat fat,
8mg cholesterol, 985mg sodium, 45g carbohydrate, 7g fiber,
16g protein*

Vegetable Quesadillas

Seaside Salmon Buns

Seaside Salmon Buns

Serves 6.

14-oz. can salmon, drained and flaked
1/4 c. green pepper, chopped
1 T. onion, chopped
2 t. lemon juice
1/2 c. low-fat mayonnaise
6 pretzel buns, split
1/2 c. low-fat shredded Cheddar cheese

Mix salmon, pepper, onion, lemon juice and mayonnaise. Pile salmon mixture onto bottom bun halves; sprinkle with cheese. Arrange salmon-topped buns on an ungreased baking sheet. Broil until lightly golden and cheese is melted. Top with remaining bun halves.

Nutrition Per Serving: 387 calories, 9g total fat, 2g sat fat, 56mg cholesterol, 962mg sodium, 48g carbohydrate, 2g fiber, 25g protein

Quick tip

A tasty apple coleslaw goes well with most any burger or sandwich. Simply toss together a large bag of coleslaw mix and a chopped Granny Smith apple. Stir in coleslaw dressing to desired consistency.

Party-Time Lasagna Buns

Makes 4 sandwiches.

4 French bread rolls
1 lb. lean ground beef
1/4 t. dried oregano
1/4 t. dried basil
8-oz. can no-salt tomato sauce
3/4 c. low-fat cottage cheese
1 c. shredded low-fat mozzarella cheese, divided
1 egg, beaten

Slice the top off each roll and set aside. Hollow out the rolls. In a skillet over medium heat, brown beef; drain. Stir in seasonings and tomato sauce. Simmer until heated through. In a bowl, mix cottage cheese, one cup mozzarella and egg. For each sandwich, spoon a layer of the beef mixture into the bottom of a bun. Spoon on a layer of cheese mixture and a layer of beef mixture. Top with remaining mozzarella. Replace bun top and wrap in aluminum foil. Place on a baking sheet and bake at 400 degrees for 30 minutes, or until cheese is melted.

Nutrition Per Serving: 432 calories, 18g total fat, 8g sat fat, 142mg cholesterol, 688mg sodium, 25g carbohydrate, 2g fiber, 42g protein

Party-Time Lasagna Buns

Sunrise Pizza

Sunrise Pizza

Serves 6.

8-oz. tube refrigerated crescent rolls
1 c. cooked ham, diced
1 c. frozen diced potatoes with onions and peppers
1 c. shredded low-fat sharp Cheddar cheese
4 eggs
3 T. milk
1/2 t. salt
1/4 t. pepper

Separate rolls into 4 rectangles. Place on an ungreased baking sheet or 12" round pizza pan. Build up edges slightly to form a crust. Firmly press perforations to seal. Sprinkle ham evenly over crust. Top with frozen vegetables and cheese. Beat eggs; stir in milk, salt and pepper. Pour egg mixture over cheese in crust. Bake at 375 degrees for 15 minutes, or until center is set.

Nutrition Per Serving: 245 calories, 12g total fat, 5g sat fat, 145mg cholesterol, 647mg sodium, 23g carbohydrate, 0g fiber, 12g protein

Open-Faced Bean & Chile Burgers

Serves 4.

16-oz. can black beans, drained and rinsed
11-oz. can corn, drained
4-oz. can green chiles
1 c. cooked brown rice
1/2 c. cornmeal
1 t. onion powder
1/4 t. garlic powder
salt to taste
2 T. oil
2 large multi-grain ciabatta rolls, split and toasted
Optional: fresh salsa

Mash beans in a large bowl; add corn, chiles, rice, cornmeal, onion powder and garlic powder. Chill well. Form mixture into 4 large patties; sprinkle with salt. Heat oil in a skillet over medium heat; add patties and cook until golden on both sides. Serve open-faced on rolls, topped with salsa, if desired.

Nutrition Per Serving: 466 calories, 9g total fat, 1g sat fat, 0mg cholesterol, 546mg sodium, 84g carbohydrate, 10g fiber, 15g protein

Open-Faced Bean & Chile Burgers

Crunchy Chicken Sandwich

Serves 6.

1 lb. ground chicken
1/4 c. low-sodium honey barbecue sauce
3/4 c. mini shredded wheat cereal, crushed
1 egg, beaten
1/8 t. salt
1/8 t. pepper
6 hamburger whole-grain buns, split

Mix all ingredients together except buns; form into 6 patties. Grill for 5 to 6 minutes per side, until no longer pink in the center. Serve on buns.

Nutrition Per Serving: 270 calories, 9g total fat, 2g sat fat, 99mg cholesterol, 391mg sodium, 29g carbohydrate, 4g fiber, 21g protein

Crunchy Chicken Sandwich

Famous Hidden Sandwich

Makes one sandwich.

1 slice rye bread
1 slice Swiss cheese
1 slice low-sodium deli turkey
1 c. lettuce, shredded
1 T. low-fat Thousand Island salad dressing
1 egg, hard-boiled, peeled and sliced
2 slices tomato
2 slices low-sodium bacon, crisply cooked
Optional: sweet pickle slices

Place bread slice on a plate. Layer with cheese and turkey slices. Mound shredded lettuce on top. Add salad dressing. Top with egg slices and tomato slices. Criss-cross bacon slices on top. Garnish with sweet pickle slices if desired.

Nutrition Per Serving: 382 calories, 22g total fat, 9g sat fat, 251mg cholesterol, 709mg sodium, 23g carbohydrate, 3g fiber, 24g protein

Quick tip

Make a quick condiment kit for your next informal get-together. Just place salt, pepper, mustard, catsup, flatware and napkins in an empty cardboard beverage carrier. So clever!

Famous Hidden Sandwich

Smokey Vegetable Pizza

Smokey Vegetable Pizza

Makes 12 servings.

1 red onion, thinly sliced into wedges

6-oz. jar marinated artichoke hearts, drained, quartered
  and marinade reserved

1 loaf frozen bread dough, thawed

1-1/2 c. smoked Gouda cheese, shredded and divided

3 roma tomatoes, sliced

4 green onions, thinly sliced

2 t. Italian seasoning

1 T. fresh basil, snipped

Place onion wedges on a lightly greased baking sheet. Brush with reserved marinade. Bake at 425 degrees for 10 minutes; remove from oven. Divide thawed dough into 12 balls. On a lightly floured surface, flatten each ball to a 4-inch circle. Place dough circles on lightly greased baking sheets; pierce with a fork. Sprinkle one cup cheese evenly over dough circles. Top each with an onion wedge, an artichoke quarter and a tomato slice. Sprinkle with sliced green onion, seasoning and remaining cheese. Bake at 425 degrees for about 10 minutes, until edges are lightly golden. Remove from oven; sprinkle with basil.

Nutrition Per Serving: *187 calories, 9g total fat, 4g sat fat, 18mg cholesterol, 331mg sodium, 20g carbohydrate, 1g fiber, 7g protein*

Cheesy Zucchini Joes

Makes 4 servings.

2 T. butter

2 zucchini, halved and sliced

1/8 t. red pepper flakes

1/8 t. garlic powder

salt and pepper to taste

1 c. marinara or spaghetti sauce

1 c. shredded low-fat mozzarella cheese

4 6-inch wheat sub rolls, split

Melt butter in a skillet over medium heat. Fry zucchini in butter until golden and slightly tender. Add seasonings. Stir in sauce. Cook and stir until sauce is heated through. For each sandwich, spoon a generous amount of zucchini mixture onto bottom half of bun. Sprinkle with cheese and replace bun top. Wrap sandwiches individually in aluminum foil. Place on a baking sheet and bake at 350 degrees for 15 minutes, or until heated through and cheese is melted.

Nutrition Per Serving: *372 calories, 14g total fat, 8g sat fat, 31mg cholesterol, 804mg sodium, 47g carbohydrate, 5g fiber, 16g protein*

Quick tip

For a cheery and pretty table accent, tuck little bright-red potted geraniums into lunch-size paper bags.

Chapter 5

Cozy & Comforting Soups & Stews

(soul-soothing bowls of goodness)

Packed with fresh and healthy ingredients, these mouthwatering soups and stews are as good for you as they are delicious! Dip into the pot for a taste of some Chicken, White Bean & Pasta Soup, scoop up a big spoonful of Rich & Meaty Chili and share a cup of Grandma's Chicken Noodle Soup with everyone at the table. So let it simmer, ladle it and pass it around. Enjoy every spoonful of these comforting, lightened-up recipes.

Salmon & Potato Chowder

Serves 6.

14-3/4 oz. can pink salmon
3 potatoes, peeled and diced
1-3/4 c. water
1 onion, chopped
4 whole peppercorns
12-oz. can evaporated milk
1 T. fresh dill, chopped
pepper to taste
Garnish: lemon wedges

Rinse salmon for one minute in a colander under cold water; set aside. Combine potatoes, water, onion and peppercorns in a large saucepan. Bring to a boil; reduce heat and simmer for 20 minutes, until potatoes are tender. Stir in milk, salmon, dill and pepper; heat through. Discard peppercorns before serving. Garnish with lemon wedges.

Nutrition Per Serving: *270 calories, 8g total fat, 3g sat fat, 75mg cholesterol, 347mg sodium, 27g carbohydrate, 2g fiber, 23g protein*

Oh-So-Easy Chili

Serves 4.

1 lb. lean ground beef
1/2 c. onion, chopped
16-oz. can low-sodium kidney beans
16-oz. can no-salt diced tomatoes
8-oz. can no-salt tomato sauce
1 T. chili powder
salt and pepper to taste
Optional: shredded low-fat Cheddar cheese

In a large skillet over medium heat, brown beef and onion; drain. Stir in undrained beans and tomatoes, tomato sauce and seasonings. Cover and simmer for 30 minutes, stirring occasionally. Top each individual serving with cheese, if desired.

Nutrition Per Serving: *344 calories, 12g total fat, 5g sat fat, 73mg cholesterol, 129mg sodium, 29g carbohydrate, 9g fiber, 29g protein*

Tomato-Basil Soup

Serves 8.

1 small onion, chopped
4 carrots, peeled and shredded
1 stalk celery, chopped
2 T. olive oil
4 c. low-sodium chicken broth
28-oz. can no-salt diced tomatoes
28-oz. can no-salt crushed tomatoes
2 T. fresh basil, chopped
salt and pepper to taste
1/2 c. fresh green beans, cut into small pieces
1/2 c. frozen peas
1 small zucchini, sliced
1 c. whole-grain penne pasta, uncooked
Optional: shredded Parmesan cheese

In a large saucepan over medium heat, sauté onion, carrots and celery in oil. Add broth. Bring to a boil; simmer for 10 minutes. Stir in undrained tomatoes and seasonings. Bring to a boil. Reduce heat to low; add beans, peas and zucchini. Cover and simmer for 25 to 30 minutes. Return to a boil; stir in pasta and cook until tender. Top with shredded cheese if desired.

Nutrition Per Serving: *167 calories, 5g total fat, 1g sat fat, 0mg cholesterol, 230mg sodium, 27g carbohydrate, 7g fiber, 7g protein*

Tomato-Basil Soup

Broccoli-Cheddar Soup

Broccoli-Cheddar Soup

Serves 6.

3/4 c. onion, finely chopped
1/4 c. butter
3/4 c. all-purpose flour
1/2 t. salt
1 t. pepper
3 c. low-sodium chicken broth
4-1/2 c. 2% milk
3 c. broccoli, chopped and cooked
3/4 c. shredded low-fat Cheddar cheese

In a large saucepan over medium heat, sauté onion in butter until tender. Stir in flour, salt and pepper; cook and stir until smooth and bubbly. Add broth and milk all at once. Cook and stir until mixture thickens and boils; add broccoli. Reduce heat and simmer, stirring constantly, until heated through. Remove from heat; stir in cheese until melted.

Nutrition Per Serving: 293 calories, 13g fat, 8g sat fat, 38mg cholesterol, 636mg sodium, 28g carbohydrate, 2g fiber, 16g protein

Grandma's Chicken Noodle Soup

Serves 8.

16-oz. pkg. thin egg noodles, uncooked
1 t. oil
12 c. low-sodium chicken broth
1/2 t. salt
1 t. poultry seasoning
1 c. celery, chopped
1 c. onion, chopped
1 c. carrot, peeled and chopped
1/3 c. cornstarch
1/4 c. cold water
4 c. cooked chicken, diced

Bring a large pot of water to a boil over medium-high heat; add noodles and oil. Cook according to package directions; drain and set aside. Combine broth, salt and poultry seasoning in another large pot; bring to a boil over medium heat. Stir in vegetables; reduce heat, cover and simmer for 15 minutes. Combine cornstarch with cold water in a small bowl; gradually add to soup, stirring constantly. Stir in chicken and noodles; heat through, about 5 to 10 minutes.

Nutrition Per Serving: 393 calories, 6g total fat, 2g sat fat, 88mg cholesterol, 333mg sodium, 53g carbohydrate, 3g fiber, 32g protein

Grandma's Chicken Noodle Soup

Iowa's Best Corn Soup

Iowa's Best Corn Soup

Makes 8 servings.

1 t. olive oil
1/2 c. onion, diced
1 clove garlic, minced
1/2 t. ground cumin
4 c. fresh corn kernels
2 new potatoes, diced
1/2 t. kosher salt
1/8 t. pepper
4 c. low-sodium vegetable broth
3/4 c. 2% milk
1 t. fresh cilantro, chopped

Heat oil in a stockpot over medium heat. Sauté onion, garlic and cumin for 5 minutes, or until onion is tender. Add remaining ingredients except milk and cilantro; bring to a boil. Reduce heat and simmer for 20 minutes, or until potatoes are tender. Add milk and cilantro; cook and stir to heat through.

Nutrition Per Serving: *130 calories, 2g total fat, 1g sat fat, 2mg cholesterol, 239mg sodium, 26g carbohydrate, 4g fiber, 4g protein*

Quick tip

Serve soup in hearty bread bowls. Simply hollow out the center of round loaves of your favorite crusty bread, leaving the bottom crust.

Kielbasa Soup

Makes 10 servings.

1 head cabbage, shredded
16-oz. pkg. Kielbasa sausage, sliced
2 16-oz. cans diced tomatoes
1 onion, chopped
2 zucchini, quartered and sliced
2 yellow squash, quartered and sliced
2 T. seasoned salt
2 cloves garlic, crushed
1 cube low-sodium beef bouillon
1 t. dried oregano
2 redskin or russet potatoes, cubed

In a stockpot, combine all ingredients except potatoes. Cover ingredients with water; bring to a boil. Cover, reduce heat and simmer for 1-1/2 to 2 hours. Add potatoes during last 30 minutes of cook time.

Nutrition Per Serving: *184 calories, 8g total fat, 3g sat fat, 31mg cholesterol, 985mg sodium, 20g carbohydrate, 4g fiber, 9g protein*

Kielbasa Soup

Chilled Melon Soup

Spicy Chicken Soup

Makes 6 servings.

1 lb. boneless, skinless chicken breasts, cubed
1 onion, chopped
1 jalapeño pepper, seeded and minced
4 cloves garlic, minced
4 carrots, peeled and thinly sliced
8 c. water
salt and pepper to taste
3/4 c. brown rice, uncooked
Garnish: lime wedges, avocado slices, shredded
    Monterey Jack cheese

Brown chicken in oil in a large soup pot over medium-high heat. Add onion, jalapeño, garlic and carrots. Cook and stir 10 minutes to soften vegetables. Add water, salt, pepper and rice. Cover and simmer for 30 minutes. Serve with desired garnishes.

Nutrition Per Serving: *195 calories, 2g total fat, 0g sat fat, 43mg cholesterol, 84mg sodium, 24g carbohydrate, 2g fiber, 20g protein*

Chilled Melon Soup

Makes 6 servings.

3 c. cantaloupe melon, peeled, seeded and chopped
1/4 c. orange juice, divided
1/4 t. salt, divided
3 c. honeydew melon, peeled, seeded and chopped
Garnish: fresh mint sprigs or orange slices

In a blender, process cantaloupe, half the juice and half the salt until smooth. Cover and refrigerate. Repeat with honeydew and remaining ingredients except garnish. Refrigerate, covered, in separate containers. To serve, pour equal amounts of each mixture at the same time on opposite sides of individual soup bowls. Garnish as desired.

Nutrition Per Serving: *62 calories, 0g total fat, 0g sat fat, 0mg cholesterol, 152mg sodium, 16g carbohydrate, 1g fiber, 1g protein*

Quick tip

Host a potluck soup supper. Ask each guest to bring their favorite soup to share. You provide a variety of whole-breads and crackers. Enjoy!

Spicy Chicken Soup

Pioneer Beef Stew

Serves 6.

14-1/2 oz. can petite diced tomatoes
1 c. water
3 T. quick-cooking tapioca, uncooked
2 t. sugar
1/2 t. salt
1/2 t. pepper
1-1/2 lbs. stew beef, cubed
3 to 4 potatoes, peeled and cubed
4 carrots, peeled and thickly sliced
1 onion, diced

In a large bowl, combine tomatoes with juice, water, tapioca, sugar, salt and pepper. Mix well; stir in remaining ingredients. Pour into a greased 3-quart casserole dish. Cover and bake at 375 degrees for 1-1/2 to 2 hours, until beef and vegetables are tender.

Nutrition Per Serving: *370 calories, 5g total fat, 2g sat fat, 70mg cholesterol, 446mg sodium, 34g carbohydrate, 4g fiber, 27g protein*

Chicken & Dumplin' Soup

Serves 10.

10-3/4 oz. can low-sodium cream of chicken soup
4 c. low-sodium chicken broth
4 boneless, skinless chicken breasts, cooked and shredded
2 16-oz. bags frozen mixed vegetables
2 12-oz. tubes refrigerated biscuits, quartered

Bring soup and broth to a slow boil in a saucepan over medium heat; whisk until smooth. Stir in chicken and

vegetables; bring to a boil. Drop biscuit quarters into soup; cover and simmer for 15 minutes. Remove from heat. Let stand 10 minutes before serving.

Nutrition Per Serving: *369 calories, 13g total fat, 3g sat fat, 30mg cholesterol, 970mg sodium, 43g carbohydrate, 4g fiber, 20g protein*

Chicken, White Bean & Pasta Soup

Makes 6 servings.

1 onion, chopped
4 carrots, peeled and sliced
4 stalks celery, sliced
2 T. olive oil
4 c. low-sodium chicken broth
3 c. water, divided
2 boneless, skinless chicken breasts, cooked and diced
2 15-1/2 oz. cans Great Northern beans, drained
6 cherry tomatoes, diced
1/2 t. dried thyme
1/2 t. dried rosemary
salt and pepper to taste
1 c. rotini pasta, uncooked
1/2 lb. baby spinach

In a large saucepan over medium heat, sauté onion, carrots and celery in oil. Add broth and 2 cups water. Bring to a boil; simmer for 10 minutes. Stir in chicken, beans, tomatoes and seasonings. Reduce heat to low; cover and simmer for 25 to 30 minutes. Return to a boil; stir in pasta. Cook until pasta is tender, about 10 minutes. Add remaining water if soup is too thick. Stir in spinach and cook for 2 minutes, or until wilted.

Nutrition Per Serving: *336 calories, 7g total fat, 1g sat fat, 23mg cholesterol, 178mg sodium, 46g carbohydrate, 11g fiber, 26g protein*

Chicken, White Bean & Pasta Soup

Taco Soup

Taco Soup

Serves 12.

1-1/2 lbs. lean ground beef
1 onion, chopped
16-oz. can kidney beans, drained
16-oz. can black beans, drained
16-oz. can pinto beans, drained
15-oz. can corn, drained
14-1/2 oz. can diced tomatoes
14-1/2 oz. can stewed tomatoes
3.8-oz. can sliced black olives, drained and diced
30-oz. can low-sodium tomato juice
1-1/2 oz. pkg. low-sodium taco seasoning mix
salt and pepper to taste
Garnish: Greek yogurt, tortilla strips, sliced black olives, sliced green onions

Brown beef and onion in a skillet over medium heat. Drain; combine with remaining ingredients except garnish in a large stockpot. Bring to a boil over medium heat; reduce heat and simmer for 30 minutes. Garnish individual portions as desired.

Nutrition Per Serving: *272 calories, 8g total fat, 3g sat fat, 36mg cholesterol, 844mg sodium, 33g carbohydrate, 9g fiber, 19g protein*

Garden-Fresh Gazpacho

Serves 12.

8 tomatoes, chopped
1 onion, finely chopped
1 cucumber, peeled and chopped
1 green pepper, chopped
2 T. fresh parsley or cilantro, chopped
1 clove garlic, finely chopped
2 stalks celery, chopped
2 T. lemon juice
salt and pepper to taste
4 c. tomato juice
4 drops hot pepper sauce
Garnish: plain Greek yogurt

Combine all ingredients except yogurt, in a large lidded container or gallon-size Mason jar. Refrigerate until well chilled. Dollop servings with yogurt.

Nutrition Per Serving: *40 calories, 0g total fat, 0g sat fat, 0mg cholesterol, 232mg sodium, 9g carbohydrate, 2g fiber, 2g protein*

Garden-Fresh Gazpacho

Bouillabaisse Gumbo

Serves 8.

16-oz. can stewed tomatoes with jalapeños
10-3/4 oz. can tomato soup
10-3/4 oz. can chicken gumbo soup
3 c. water
1 c. sweet potato, peeled and chopped
1/4 c. celery, chopped
1/4 c. carrots, peeled and chopped
1/3 c. green onions, chopped
1 T. fresh parsley, chopped
1 T. fresh cilantro, chopped
1 T. low-sodium Worcestershire sauce
1 clove garlic, minced
1 bay leaf
1/2 lb. uncooked medium shrimp, cleaned
8-oz. can minced clams
1/4 to 1/2 t. dried oregano
salt and pepper to taste

In a large pot, combine all ingredients except shrimp, clams, oregano, salt and pepper. Cover and simmer over medium-low heat for 30 minutes, or until vegetables are tender. Add shrimp and undrained clams; simmer 10 minutes. Stir in remaining ingredients. Remove bay leaf before serving.

Nutrition Per Serving: *143 calories, 2g total fat, 0g sat fat, 62mg cholesterol, 701mg sodium, 17g carbohydrate, 2g fiber, 15g protein*

Rich & Meaty Chili

Serves 8.

1 lb. lean ground beef
1/2 c. onion, chopped
1 T. butter
2 15-1/2 oz. cans no-salt kidney beans
2 15-oz. cans no-salt chili beans
4 c. diced tomatoes
6-oz. can tomato paste
1-1/2 c. water
1 c. celery, chopped
1 c. green pepper, chopped
2 to 3 t. chili powder
1/2 t. dried oregano
1/2 t. salt
1/4 t. pepper
1/8 t. hot pepper sauce
1 bay leaf

In a Dutch oven over medium-high heat, brown ground beef with onion in butter; drain. Stir in remaining ingredients. Bring to a boil; reduce heat and simmer for one hour. Remove bay leaf before serving.

Nutrition Per Serving: *375 calories, 9g total fat, 3g sat fat, 40mg cholesterol, 583mg sodium, 51g carbohydrate, 16g fiber, 27g protein*

Bouillabaisse Gumbo

Rich & Meaty Chili

Vegetable Goodness Minestrone

Makes 4 servings.

1-1/4 c. whole-wheat elbow macaroni or small shell pasta, uncooked
16-oz. pkg. frozen mixed vegetables
2 c. low-sodium vegetable broth
14-1/2 oz. can diced tomatoes
15-1/2 oz. can kidney beans, drained and rinsed
2 T. fresh parsley, chopped, or 2 t. dried parsley
1 t. Italian seasoning
1/4 t. pepper

Cook macaroni or pasta according to package instructions; drain. Meanwhile, in a separate large saucepan over medium heat, cook frozen vegetables in broth for 15 minutes, or until tender. Do not drain. Add tomatoes with juice and remaining ingredients; stir in cooked macaroni or pasta. Reduce heat to low; heat through.

Nutrition Per Serving: *315 calories, 2g total fat, 0g sat fat, 0mg cholesterol, 663mg sodium, 65g carbohydrate, 15g fiber, 15g protein*

Bean & Butternut Soup

Serves 10.

1 lb. dried navy beans
8 c. water
4 t. ham soup base
1 lb. meaty ham shanks
1 c. onion, chopped
1 c. celery, chopped
2 lbs. butternut squash, peeled, cubed and divided
pepper to taste

In a 5-quart Dutch oven, combine beans, water and soup base. Cover and refrigerate overnight. The next day, without draining, add ham shanks, onion, celery, half the squash cubes and pepper. Bring to a boil over high heat. Reduce heat to low; cover and simmer for 1-1/2 hours. Remove ham shanks and let cool slightly; remove meat from the bones and chop. Partially mash beans with a potato masher. Add chopped ham and remaining squash cubes to the pot. Simmer, covered, for an additional 20 minutes, or until squash is tender.

Nutrition Per Serving: *284 calories, 5g total fat, 2g sat fat, 28mg cholesterol, 656mg sodium, 40g carbohydrate, 13g fiber, 21g protein*

Nana's Potato Soup

Serves 8.

1/2 c. butter
10 T. all-purpose flour
4 14-1/2 oz. cans low-sodium chicken broth
1 T. fresh chives, chopped
1 T. fresh parsley, chopped
2 c. whole milk
2 c. 2% milk
8 potatoes, peeled, cubed and cooked
salt and pepper to taste
Garnish: shredded Cheddar cheese, chopped chives

Melt butter in a Dutch oven over medium heat. Stir in flour, one tablespoon at a time, until smooth. Add broth, chives and parsley; stir until thickened. Add milk, stirring until well mixed. Stir in potatoes and heat through; sprinkle to taste with salt and pepper. Garnish as desired.

Nutrition Per Serving: *405 calories, 16g total fat, 10g sat fat, 42mg cholesterol, 136mg sodium, 56g carbohydrate, 5g fiber, 14g protein*

Nana's Potato Soup

Chicken Cacciatore Soup

Serves 8.

1 c. rotini pasta, uncooked
3 14-1/2 oz. cans low-sodium vegetable broth, divided
1/2 lb. boneless, skinless chicken breasts, cut into
  bite-size pieces
30-oz. jar extra-chunky spaghetti sauce with mushrooms
14-1/2 oz. can no-salt stewed tomatoes, chopped
1 zucchini, sliced
1 onion, chopped
2 cloves garlic, chopped
1/2 t. Italian seasoning
1 T. red wine

Cook rotini according to package directions, substituting one can broth for part of the water; drain and set aside. Combine remaining ingredients in a large saucepan. Simmer 20 to 30 minutes, until chicken is cooked through and vegetables are tender. Stir in rotini; heat through.

Nutrition Per Serving: *114 calories, 1g total fat, 0g sat fat, 16mg cholesterol, 117mg sodium, 17g carbohydrate, 2g fiber, 9g protein*

Kale Soup

Makes 4 servings.

8 c. chicken broth
1-1/2 lbs. fresh kale, ribs discarded and leaves
  finely chopped
1/2 c. onion, minced
4 eggs, beaten
1/4 c. lemon juice
Garnish: shredded Parmesan cheese

Bring broth to a boil in a heavy saucepan over medium heat. Add kale and onion. Reduce heat to medium-low and simmer until kale is tender, about 20 minutes.

Remove pan from heat; allow mixture to cool to room temperature. Once cooled whisk together eggs and lemon juice in a bowl; whisk into soup. Warm soup over very low heat; do not boil. Ladle soup into bowls. Serve with Parmesan cheese on the side.

Nutrition Per Serving: *162 calories, 6g total fat, 2g sat fat, 211mg cholesterol, 826mg sodium, 14g carbohydrate, 4g fiber, 15g protein*

Chicken & Wild Rice Soup

Makes 8 servings.

4 boneless, skinless chicken breasts, cut into large cubes
9 c. water
3 cloves garlic, minced
3 T. butter
2 shallots, sliced
1-1/2 c. baby portabella mushrooms, sliced
8-oz. pkg. wild rice, uncooked
1/2 c. whole milk
salt and pepper to taste
Garnish: sliced green onions

Combine chicken and water in a large saucepan. Bring to a boil over medium-high heat; reduce heat to low. Cover and simmer for 20 minutes. Remove chicken to a bowl, reserving broth. Let chicken cool. Meanwhile, in a large stockpot over medium heat, sauté garlic in butter until fragrant. Add shallots and mushrooms; cook until almost tender. Add rice; cook and stir for 2 to 3 minutes. Add 7 cups reserved broth. Bring to a boil; reduce heat to medium-low. Cover and cook, stirring occasionally, for 20 minutes. Shred chicken; add chicken to soup. Cover and simmer for 15 to 20 minutes, until most of broth is absorbed. If more liquid is needed, add remaining broth, one cup at a time, to desired consistency. Stir in milk; bring to a boil. Reduce heat to medium-low and simmer for another 15 to 20 minutes. Add salt and pepper to taste. Garnish with sliced green onions.

Nutrition Per Serving: *216 calories, 6g total fat, 3g sat fat, 47mg cholesterol, 48mg sodium, 23g carbohydrate, 2g fiber, 19g protein*

Chicken & Wild Rice Soup

Vegetable Soup

Serves 6.

8 c. water
1 t. salt
1/4 t. pepper
1 t. sugar
6 carrots, peeled and diced
3 stalks celery, diced
3 onions, diced
1/4 head cabbage, shredded
1 c. tomatoes, diced
4 sprigs fresh parsley
2 cubes low-sodium vegetable bouillon

In a stockpot over medium-high heat, combine water, salt, pepper and sugar. Bring to a boil. Add vegetables and parsley. Reduce heat to medium and simmer one hour. Add bouillon cubes; remove from heat and stir until bouillon is completely dissolved. Serve hot.

Nutrition Per Serving: *91 calories, 2g total fat, 1g sat fat, 0mg cholesterol, 560mg sodium, 18g carbohydrate, 5g fiber, 3g protein*

Stuffed Pepper Soup

Makes 6 servings.

1 lb. lean ground beef
1/2 c. onion, diced
28-oz. can diced tomatoes
1 green pepper, diced
14-oz. can beef broth
2 c. cooked rice
salt and pepper to taste

In a stockpot over medium heat, brown beef with onion; drain. Add tomatoes with juice and remaining ingredients. Reduce heat to medium-low. Simmer until green pepper is tender, about 30 minutes.

Nutrition Per Serving: *246 calories, 8g total fat, 3g sat fat, 49mg cholesterol, 544mg sodium, 23g carbohydrate, 3g fiber, 19g protein*

Old-Fashioned Tomato Soup

Serves 6.

32-oz. can diced tomatoes
1 c. chicken broth
1 T. butter
2 T. sugar
1 T. green onion, chopped
1/8 t. baking soda
1 c. whole milk
1 c. 2% milk

Combine undrained tomatoes, broth, butter, sugar, onion and baking soda in a large saucepan. Simmer over low heat for one hour. Warm milk in a double boiler; add to hot tomato mixture. Blend well. Garnish as desired.

Nutrition Per Serving: *122 calories, 4g total fat, 2g sat fat, 12mg cholesterol, 419mg sodium, 17g carbohydrate, 3g fiber, 5g protein*

Quick tip

Garnishes make soups and stews look extra delicious! Add little toasted bagel slices, a sprinkling of cheese or fresh herbs just before serving.

Old-Fashioned Tomato Soup

Summer Squash Chowder
Makes 4 servings.

3 slices bacon, chopped
1 onion, finely diced
1 clove garlic, minced
1 yellow or red pepper, finely diced
2 T. all-purpose flour
14-1/2 oz. can low-sodium vegetable broth, divided
5-oz. can evaporated milk
4 zucchini, diced
2 yellow squash, diced
1 t. white wine Worcestershire sauce
1/2 t. hot pepper sauce
3/4 t. dried thyme
1/2 t. salt
1 c. fresh corn kernels
2 T. lemon juice
1/2 c. fresh parsley, finely chopped
pepper to taste

In a soup pot over medium heat, cook bacon until crisp. Set aside bacon and drain leaving 1 T. of drippings in pot. Add onion, garlic and yellow or red pepper into soup pot; sauté 5 minutes. Sprinkle flour evenly over vegetables and cook one minute stirring constantly. Add 1/2 cup broth, stirring well to blend. Cook over medium heat until thickened. Pour in remaining broth, milk, zucchini, squash, sauces, thyme and salt. Bring to a boil. Reduce heat and simmer, covered, 15 minutes, stirring occasionally. Add corn to a saucepan; cover with water. Cook over medium heat 5 minutes. Drain and stir into soup mixture. Add reserved bacon, juice and parsley. Heat through and add pepper to taste.

Nutrition Per Serving: *263 calories, 14g total fat, 5g sat fat, 26mg cholesterol, 632mg sodium, 28g carbohydrate, 6g fiber, 11g protein*

Hearty Hamburger Stew
Makes 4 servings.

1 lb. lean ground beef
1 onion, chopped
1/2 c. celery, chopped
5-1/2 c. no-salt tomato juice
1 c. water
1/2 c. pearled barley, uncooked
2 t. chili powder
salt and pepper to taste

In a large saucepan over medium heat, cook beef, onion and celery until beef is no longer pink. Drain; stir in remaining ingredients. Bring to a boil; reduce heat to low. Cover and simmer, stirring occasionally, for 50 minutes, or until barley is tender.

Nutrition Per Serving: *355 calories, 12g total fat, 5g sat fat, 73mg cholesterol, 411mg sodium, 37g carbohydrate, 6g fiber, 28g protein*

Chicken Noodle Gumbo
Serves 10.

2 lbs. boneless, skinless chicken breasts, cut into cubes
4 16-oz. cans low-sodium chicken broth
15-oz. can diced tomatoes
32-oz. pkg. frozen okra, corn, celery and red pepper mixed vegetables
8-oz. pkg. bowtie whole-wheat pasta, uncooked
1/2 t. garlic powder
salt and pepper to taste

Place chicken, broth and tomatoes in a large soup pot. Bring to a boil over medium heat. Reduce heat; simmer 10 minutes. Add frozen vegetables, uncooked pasta and seasonings. Return to a boil. Cover and simmer one hour.

Nutrition Per Serving: *258 calories, 2g total fat, 1g sat fat, 2mg cholesterol, 198mg sodium, 32g carbohydrate, 5g fiber, 28g protein*

Hearty Hamburger Stew

Veggie Patch Stew

Makes 6 servings.

3 zucchini, sliced
3 yellow squash, sliced
2 onions, chopped
2 tomatoes, chopped
1 eggplant, peeled and cubed
1 green pepper, chopped
1 clove garlic, minced
1 T. butter, softened
1 t. hot pepper sauce
1/2 t. curry powder
1 t. chili powder
salt and pepper to taste
Garnish: shredded low-fat mozzarella cheese

Place all vegetables in a large Dutch oven over low heat. Stir in remaining ingredients except cheese. Cover and simmer for one hour, stirring frequently. Do not add any liquid, as vegetables make their own juices. Top portions with cheese before serving.

Nutrition Per Serving: 94 calories, 3g total fat, 1g sat fat, 5mg cholesterol, 45mg sodium, 17g carbohydrate, 6g fiber, 4g protein

Veggie Patch Stew

Chicken & Orzo Soup

Serves 4.

1 T. olive oil
1 leek, halved lengthwise and sliced 1/2-inch thick
1 stalk celery, sliced
3/4 lb. boneless, skinless chicken thighs
6 c. low-sodium chicken broth
salt and pepper to taste
1/2 c. orzo pasta, uncooked
1/4 c. fresh dill, chopped
Garnish: lemon wedges

Heat oil in a large soup pot over medium heat. Add leek and celery; cook, stirring often, until vegetables are tender, 5 to 8 minutes. Add chicken and broth; season with salt and pepper. Bring to a boil; reduce heat to medium-low. Cover and simmer until chicken juices are no longer pink, about 15 to 20 minutes. Remove chicken to a plate, reserving broth in soup pot. Let chicken cool; chop. Meanwhile, return broth to a boil. Stir in orzo and cook until tender, about 8 minutes. Stir in chicken and dill; let stand several minutes, until heated through. Serve bowls of soup with lemon wedges for squeezing.

Nutrition Per Serving: 375 calories, 18g total fat, 5g sat fat, 70mg cholesterol, 173mg sodium, 27g carbohydrate, 1g fiber, 25g protein

Quick tip

Fill a basket with the fixin's for a simple supper like a favorite soup with bread and cheese. Deliver to new parents or an elderly friend. How thoughtful!

Chicken & Orzo Soup

Creamy Asparagus Soup

Creamy Asparagus Soup

Makes 2 servings.

1 T. butter
1 lb. asparagus, trimmed and chopped
1 T. onion, minced
2 T. celery, chopped
14-1/2 oz. can low-sodium chicken broth
salt and pepper to taste
3/4 c. whole milk

Melt butter in a stock pot. Add asparagus, onion and celery and cook until crisp-tender. Add remaining ingredients except milk. Bring to a boil; reduce heat and simmer 5 to 7 minutes. Working in small batches, ladle asparagus mixture into a blender. Add milk and purée. Return mixture to soup pot and heat through without boiling. Garnish as desired.

Nutrition Per Serving: 126 calories, 4g total fat, 2g sat fat, 10mg cholesterol, 690mg sodium, 16g carbohydrate, 4g fiber, 12g protein

Beef Stew & Biscuits

Serves 6.

1 lb. lean ground beef
1/4 c. onion, chopped
1/4 t. dried basil
3-1/2 c. frozen mixed vegetables
2 8-oz. cans no-salt tomato sauce
1 c. sharp low-fat Cheddar cheese, cubed
12-oz. tube refrigerated biscuits

In a skillet over medium heat, brown beef and onion; drain. Add basil, mixed vegetables and tomato sauce; mix well. Cover and simmer for 5 minutes. Fold in cheese cubes; pour into an ungreased 2-quart casserole dish. Arrange biscuits on top. Bake, uncovered, at 375 degrees for 25 minutes, or until biscuits are golden.

Nutrition Per Serving: 437 calories, 15g total fat, 7g sat fat, 53mg cholesterol, 708mg sodium, 45g carbohydrate, 7g fiber, 26g protein

Chill-Chaser Pork Stew

Chill-Chaser Pork Stew

Serves 6.

2 to 2-1/2 lbs. pork steaks, cubed
1 T. olive oil
2 sweet onions, chopped
2 green peppers, chopped
2 cloves garlic, minced
salt and pepper to taste
6-oz. can tomato paste
28-oz. can diced tomatoes
8-oz. can sliced mushrooms, drained

In a Dutch oven over medium heat, sauté pork in oil until browned. Add onions, green peppers, garlic, salt and pepper. Cover; cook over medium heat until pork is tender. Add tomato paste, tomatoes with juice and mushrooms; bring to a boil. Reduce heat to low; simmer for one hour, stirring often.

Nutrition Per Serving: 361 calories, 19g total fat, 6g sat fat, 93mg cholesterol, 882mg sodium, 19g carbohydrate, 6g fiber, 29g protein

Chicken Enchilada Soup

Chicken Enchilada Soup

Serves 6.

1 onion, chopped
1 clove garlic, pressed
2 t. oil
14-1/2 oz. can low-sodium beef broth
14-1/2 oz. can low- sodium chicken broth
10-3/4 oz. can low- sodium cream of chicken soup
1-1/2 c. water
12-1/2 oz. can chicken, drained
4-oz. can chopped green chiles
2 t. low-sodium Worcestershire sauce
1 T. steak sauce
1 t. ground cumin
1 t. chili powder
1/8 t. pepper
6 corn tortillas, cut into strips
1 c. shredded low-fat Cheddar cheese

In a stockpot over medium heat, sauté onion and garlic in oil. Add remaining ingredients except tortilla strips and cheese; bring to a boil. Cover; reduce heat and simmer for one hour, stirring occasionally. Uncover and stir in tortilla strips and cheese. Simmer an additional 10 minutes.

Nutrition Per Serving: *261 calories, 9g total fat, 3g sat fat, 36mg cholesterol, 533mg sodium, 20g carbohydrate, 2g fiber, 24g protein*

Old-Fashioned Ham & Bean Soup

Serves 6.

2 meaty ham hocks or 1 meaty ham bone
16-oz. pkg. dried navy beans
1 c. cooked ham, chopped
1/2 to 3/4 c. onion, quartered and sliced
3 stalks celery, chopped
1/2 c. carrot, peeled and grated
2 bay leaves
1/2 t. garlic powder
1/4 t. pepper
1/2 t. dried parsley
1/8 t. dried thyme

The night before, cover ham hocks or ham bone with water in a large stockpot. Simmer over medium heat until tender. Remove ham hocks or bone from stockpot, reserving broth; slice off ham. Refrigerate reserved broth and meat overnight. Cover beans with water in a bowl and let stand overnight. The next day, drain beans and set aside. Discard fat from top of reserved broth; add beans, ham, and remaining ingredients to broth. Bring to a boil. Reduce heat; simmer until beans are tender and soup is desired thickness, about one hour. Discard bay leaves.

Nutrition Per Serving: *372 calories, 6g total fat, 2g sat fat, 44mg cholesterol, 365mg sodium, 49g carbohydrate, 19g fiber, 32g protein*

Chicken Corn Chowder

Serves 8.

1-1/2 c. 2% milk
10-1/2 oz. can low-sodium chicken broth
10-3/4 oz. can low-sodium cream of chicken soup
10-3/4 oz. can low-sodium cream of potato soup
10-oz. can chicken, drained
1/3 c. green onion, chopped
11-oz. can sweet corn & diced peppers
4-oz. can chopped green chiles, drained
8-oz. pkg. low-fat shredded Cheddar cheese

Mix together all ingredients except cheese in a stockpot. Cook over low heat, stirring frequently, for 15 minutes, or until heated through. Add cheese; stir until melted.

Nutrition Per Serving: 279 calories, 14g total fat, 8g sat fat, 56mg cholesterol, 764mg sodium, 20g carbohydrate, 1g fiber, 19g protein

Kansas Beef Stew

Makes 4 servings.

1-1/4 lbs. stew beef, cubed
2 T. olive oil
1/2 c. onion, chopped
1-1/2 t. garlic powder
1/4 t. pepper
1 c. water
10-oz. can diced tomatoes with green chiles
1 T. ground cumin
1/2 t. salt

In a deep skillet over medium heat, brown beef on all sides in oil. Remove beef to a bowl. Add onion, garlic powder and pepper to skillet; cook until onion is translucent. Drain. Return beef to skillet; add water. Bring to a boil; reduce heat to low. Cover and simmer for one hour, stirring occasionally. Stir in tomatoes with juice, cumin and salt. Return stew to a boil and simmer an additional 30 minutes, or until beef is very tender.

Nutrition Per Serving: 353 calories, 13g total fat, 3g sat fat, 87mg cholesterol, 729mg sodium, 4g carbohydrate, 1g fiber, 30g protein

Chicken Corn Chowder

Chapter 6

Fresh-Baked Breads & Muffins

(homemade and whole-grain)

Whether you prefer a thick slice of rye bread, a savory buttermilk scone, a healthy carrot muffin or a perfect piece of coffee cake, you'll enjoy every crumb of these baked goodies knowing they are full of homemade goodness. Reach for a swirled Buttermilk Cinnamon Roll, fill a basket with Mile-High Biscuits and round out your dinner with Granny's Country Cornbread. These comforting recipes from your kitchen are sure to please.

Mom's Applesauce Muffins

Mom's Applesauce Muffins

Makes 12 muffins. Serves 12.

1/2 c. butter, softened
1 c. sugar
1 egg, beaten
1 c. applesauce
1 t. cinnamon
1/2 t. ground cloves
1 t. baking soda
1/4 t. salt
2 c. all-purpose flour
1 c. raisins

Combine all ingredients; stir until moistened. Spoon batter into 12 paper-lined muffin cups, filling 3/4 full. Sprinkle with Crumb Topping. Bake at 350 degrees for 25 to 30 minutes.

Crumb Topping:

1/2 c. butter
3/4 c. all-purpose flour
3/4 c. quick-cooking oats, uncooked
1/4 c. brown sugar, packed
2 t. cinnamon

Blend all ingredients until crumbly.

Nutrition Per Serving: 354 calories, 14g total fat, 10g sat fat, 52mg cholesterol, 270mg sodium, 58g carbohydrate, 2g fiber, 4g protein

Best-Ever Banana Bread

Serves 12.

1/2 c. butter
1 c. sugar
2 eggs
3/4 c. ripe banana, mashed
1-1/4 c. cake flour
3/4 t. baking soda
1/2 t. salt

In a large bowl, blend butter and sugar well. Add eggs, one at a time, beating well after each; stir in banana and set aside. Stir together flour, baking soda and salt in a separate bowl; add to butter mixture and mix well. Pour into 6 greased 5-1/2"x3" mini loaf pans. Bake loaves at 350 degrees for 30 to 35 minutes or until done.

Nutrition Per Serving: 176 calories, 7g total fat, 5g sat fat, 24mg cholesterol, 212mg sodium, 29g carbohydrate, 0g fiber, 2g protein

Best-Ever Banana Bread

Cinnamon Apple-Raisin Muffins
Makes 12 muffins. Serves 12.

1 c. all-purpose flour
1 c. whole-wheat flour
3/4 t. baking soda
1/2 t. salt
1 t. cinnamon
3/4 c. unsweetened applesauce
1/4 c. oil
1/2 c. sugar
2 eggs, beaten
1 t. vanilla extract
2 c. apples, peeled, cored and diced
1 c. raisins
1/2 c. chopped walnuts

In a bowl, stir together flours, baking soda, salt and cinnamon; set aside. In a separate large bowl, beat applesauce, oil and sugar with an electric mixer on low speed for 2 minutes. Add eggs and vanilla; beat for one minute and set aside. Add flour mixture to applesauce mixture; stir just until moist. Fold in remaining ingredients. Spoon batter into 12 paper-lined muffin cups, filling 2/3 full. Bake at 400 degrees for 25 to 30 minutes, until a toothpick inserted in center tests clean. Remove muffins from tin to a wire rack; serve warm or cooled.

Nutrition Per Serving: 243 calories, 9g total fat, 1g sat fat, 24mg cholesterol, 170mg sodium, 38g carbohydrate, 2g fiber, 2g protein

Sweet Fruit & Almond Scones
Serves 10.

2 c. all-purpose flour
1/4 c. sugar, divided
1 T. baking powder
1/4 t. salt
6 T. chilled butter, diced
2 eggs, lightly beaten
1/2 c. plus 1 T. 2% milk, divided
1/2 c. dried cranberries and blueberries
1/2 c. sliced toasted almonds

In a large bowl, sift together flour, 3 tablespoons sugar, baking powder and salt; set aside. Use a fork or pastry blender to cut in butter until very small pieces form. Make a well in the center; set aside. In a separate bowl, whisk eggs and 1/2 cup milk together. Pour egg mixture into well in flour mixture. Stir lightly with a fork until dough comes together. Add berries and nuts; mix together. Turn out dough onto a lightly floured surface. With floured hands, gently pat dough into an 8-inch circle, about 3/8-inch thick. Cut circle into 10 wedges; transfer to a parchment paper-lined baking sheet. Brush tops with remaining milk and sprinkle with remaining sugar. Bake at 400 degrees for 15 to 20 minutes, until golden. Cool on a wire rack. Drizzle with Powdered Sugar Frosting.

Powdered Sugar Frosting:
1 c. powdered sugar
1 T. milk

Mix together to the consistency of heavy cream.

Nutrition Per Serving: 223 calories, 11g total fat, 5g sat fat, 48mg cholesterol, 302mg sodium, 29g carbohydrate, 1g fiber, 5g protein

Sweet Fruit & Almond Scones

Fresh-Baked Breads & Muffins

Refrigerator Pumpkin Muffins

Refrigerator Pumpkin Muffins

Serves 30.

2 c. bran & raisin cereal
2 c. buttermilk
2 c. cooked pumpkin purée, or 15-oz. can pumpkin
1/3 c. butter, melted and slightly cooled
2 eggs, beaten
1-1/2 c. all-purpose flour
1 c. whole-wheat flour
1-1/2 c. sugar
2 t. baking powder
1 t. baking soda
1 t. cinnamon
1/2 t. ginger
1/4 t. ground cloves
3 T. ground flax seed

Combine cereal and buttermilk in a large bowl; let stand 5 minutes. Add pumpkin, butter and eggs; mix well. In a separate large bowl, mix together flours, sugar, baking powder, baking soda, spices and flax seed. Add pumpkin mixture to flour mixture; stir until completely moistened. Batter may be baked immediately, or stored up to 2 days in a tightly covered container in the refrigerator. To bake, spoon batter into lightly greased or paper-lined muffin cups, filling 3/4 full. Bake at 400 degrees for 18 to 20 minutes, until muffin tops are firm to the touch.

Nutrition Per Serving: *114 calories, 3g total fat, 1g sat fat, 10mg cholesterol, 129mg sodium, 22g carbohydrate, 2g fiber, 2g protein*

Low-Fat Chocolate Oat Muffins

Serves 12.

2 c. oat flour
1/3 c. brown sugar, packed
1/3 c. baking cocoa
2 t. baking powder
1/2 t. baking soda
1/2 t. salt
1 c. dark chocolate chips
2/3 c. zucchini, finely grated
1 c. non-fat milk
1/3 c. honey
2 egg whites, beaten
Garnish: oatmeal

In a bowl, combine flour, brown sugar, baking cocoa, baking powder, baking soda and salt. Mix well; gently stir in chocolate chips. In a separate large bowl, combine remaining ingredients; mix well. Add flour mixture to zucchini mixture; stir only until well combined. Spoon batter into muffin cups sprayed with non-stick vegetable spray, filling cups 2/3 full. Sprinkle oatmeal on top of muffins. Bake at 400 degrees for 18 to 20 minutes, until a toothpick tests clean. Cool muffin tin on a wire rack for 10 minutes; remove muffins from tin.

Nutrition Per Serving: *240 calories, 7g total fat, 4g sat fat, 2mg cholesterol, 313mg sodium, 37g carbohydrate, 5g fiber, 8g protein*

Low-Fat Chocolate Oat Muffins

Granny's Country Cornbread

Granny's Country Cornbread

Makes 8 servings.

1-1/4 c. cornmeal
3/4 c. all-purpose flour
5 T. sugar
2 t. baking powder
1/2 t. salt
1 c. buttermilk
1/3 c. oil
1 egg, beaten
1 c. shredded low-fat sharp Cheddar cheese
1 c. canned corn, drained
1 T. jalapeño pepper, minced

Mix together cornmeal, flour, sugar, baking powder and salt in a large bowl. Make a well in center; pour in buttermilk, oil and egg. Stir mixture just until ingredients are lightly moistened. Fold in cheese, corn and jalapeño; pour into a greased 8" cast-iron skillet. Bake at 375 degrees for 20 minutes, or until a tester inserted in the center comes out clean. Let cool slightly; cut into 8 wedges.

Nutrition Per Serving: 271 calories, 11g total fat, 2g sat fat, 19mg cholesterol, 517mg sodium, 36g carbohydrate, 1g fiber, 8g protein

Quick tip

Making honey butter is easy and delicious on any bread. Simply whip together one tablespoon honey to 1/2 cup butter. Yummy!

Swedish Rye Bread

Serves 24.

2 envs. active dry yeast
3 c. warm water
1 T. sugar
9 c. all-purpose flour, divided
2-1/2 c. rye flour
1/2 c. brown sugar, packed
1 c. molasses
1 T. butter
2 t. salt
3/4 c. boiling water

In a large bowl, dissolve yeast in very warm water, about 110 to 115 degrees. Let stand for 5 minutes. Add sugar and 3 cups all-purpose flour; set aside. In a separate bowl, mix rye flour, brown sugar, molasses, butter, salt and boiling water. Stir well; add rye flour mixture to yeast mixture. Stir in enough of remaining all-purpose flour to form dough. Place dough in a greased bowl; turn to coat and cover with a tea towel. Let rise until dough doubles in size, 1-1/2 to 2 hours. Punch down dough. Divide dough into 4 balls; place in 4 greased 9"x5" loaf pans or on greased baking sheets. Cover and let rise again, an additional 1-1/2 to 2 hours. Bake at 350 degrees for 25 to 30 minutes, until golden and loaves sound hollow when tapped. Makes 4 loaves.

Nutrition Per Serving: 254 calories, 1g total fat, 0g sat fat, 1mg cholesterol, 214mg sodium, 55g carbohydrate, 2g fiber, 7g protein

Swedish Rye Bread

Orange-Glazed Blueberry Scones

Serves 12.

2 c. plus 2 T. all-purpose flour, divided
1 T. baking powder
1 t. salt
1/3 c. sugar
1/2 c. chilled butter, diced
3/4 c. buttermilk
1 egg, beaten
2 c. fresh blueberries

In a large bowl, sift together 2 cups flour, baking powder, salt and sugar; mix well. Cut in butter with a fork until crumbs form. In a separate bowl, whisk together buttermilk and egg; add to flour mixture. Mix just to incorporate without overworking the dough. In another bowl, toss berries in remaining flour; gently fold berries into batter. Drop large tablespoons of batter onto ungreased baking sheets. Bake at 400 degrees for 15 to 20 minutes, until golden. Cool scones on a wire rack. Drizzle or brush Orange Glaze over scones. Let stand until glaze becomes hazy and hardened.

Orange Glaze:

1 T. butter, diced
2 c. powdered sugar
3 T. orange juice

Combine butter, sugar and enough juice for desired consistency. Beat until smooth.

Nutrition Per Serving: *262 calories, 8g total fat, 5g sat fat, 35mg cholesterol, 426mg sodium, 45g carbohydrate, 1g fiber, 3g protein*

Buttermilk Cinnamon Rolls

Serves 15.

3 c. all-purpose flour
4 t. baking powder
1/4 t. baking soda
1 t. salt
1/2 c. cold butter
1-1/2 c. buttermilk
1/4 c. butter, softened
1/2 c. sugar
1 t. cinnamon

In a large bowl, combine first 4 ingredients; cut in cold butter until crumbs form. Stir in buttermilk until well blended; knead dough on a lightly floured surface for 4 to 5 minutes. Roll out to 1/4-inch thickness; spread softened butter over dough to edges. In a small bowl, mix sugar and cinnamon; sprinkle over dough. Roll up jelly-roll style; cut into 1/2-inch slices. Place on 2 greased baking sheets; bake at 400 degrees for 10 to 12 minutes.

Nutrition Per Serving: *194 calories, 8g total fat, 6g sat fat, 25mg cholesterol, 424mg sodium, 25g carbohydrate, 0g fiber, 3g protein*

Quick tip

Freeze those yummy leftover breads and rolls for later by placing them on paper plates and covering with a plastic bag. When time to serve, just remove the bag and heat in the microwave. What a treat!

Buttermilk Cinnamon Rolls

Blackberry Buckle

Blackberry Buckle

Makes 9 servings.

2 c. all-purpose flour
2-1/2 t. baking powder
1/4 t. salt
1/2 c. butter
3/4 c. sugar
1 egg, beaten
1/2 c. milk
2 c. blackberries

Stir together flour, baking powder and salt; set aside. In a separate bowl, blend butter and sugar until light and fluffy. Add egg and beat well. Add flour mixture and milk alternately to egg mixture, beating until smooth. Pour into a greased 9"x9" baking pan; top with blackberries and Crumb Topping. Bake at 350 degrees for 50 to 60 minutes, or until golden. Serve warm.

Crumb Topping:

1/2 c. all-purpose flour
1/2 c. sugar
1/2 t. cinnamon
1/4 c. butter

Sift together flour, sugar and cinnamon. Cut in butter until mixture resembles coarse crumbs.

Nutrition Per Serving: *373 calories, 14g total fat, 10g sat fat, 57mg cholesterol, 353mg sodium, 55g carbohydrate, 1g fiber, 4g protein*

Peanut Butter-Banana Muffins

Serves 18.

2-1/3 c. all-purpose flour
1-1/2 t. baking powder
1 t. baking soda
1/4 t. salt
1/3 c. butter, softened
1/4 c. creamy peanut butter
1/2 c. sugar
2 eggs
1 c. milk
2 ripe bananas, mashed

Combine flour, baking powder, baking soda and salt in a bowl; set aside. In a separate large bowl, combine butter and peanut butter; beat with an electric mixer on low speed until smooth. Add sugar; beat until light and fluffy, about 3 minutes. Beat in eggs. Alternately beat in flour mixture, milk and bananas with mixer on low speed until blended. Spoon batter evenly into 18 paper-lined or greased muffin cups, filling 2/3 full. Bake at 400 degrees for 20 minutes, or until a toothpick inserted in center tests clean. Cool muffins in tins on a wire rack for 10 minutes; turn out muffins and cool muffins completely.

Nutrition Per Serving: *147 calories, 5g total fat, 3g sat fat, 26mg cholesterol, 187mg sodium, 21g carbohydrate, 1g fiber, 3g protein*

Quick tip

A wire basket full of brown eggs make a terrific farm-style breakfast centerpiece. Place the centerpiece on a favorite cloth placemat.

Sweet Avocado Muffins

Serves 12.

2 c. all-purpose flour
1 t. baking powder
1 t. baking soda
1/2 t. sea salt
2 eggs
1 c. sugar
1/2 c. canola oil
1-1/2 c. very ripe avocado, halved, pitted and mashed
1 T. lime juice
1-1/4 t. vanilla extract
Optional: 1/2 c. chopped walnuts

In a large bowl, mix together flour, baking powder, baking soda and salt; set aside. In a separate bowl, beat eggs and sugar until fluffy; stir in oil, avocado, lime juice and vanilla. Add oil mixture to flour mixture; stir just until combined. Spoon batter into 12 paper-lined muffin cups, filling 2/3 full. Sprinkle with walnuts, if desired. Bake at 350 degrees for 15 to 20 minutes, until a toothpick inserted in center tests clean. Remove muffins to a wire rack; let cool.

Nutrition Per Serving: *239 calories, 12g total fat, 1g sat fat, 24mg cholesterol, 233mg sodium, 31g carbohydrate, 0g fiber, 3g protein*

Farmhouse Bread

Serves 24.

2 T. active dry yeast
1 c. warm water, 110 to 115 degrees
4 c. warm 2% milk
1/2 c. oil
6 T. sugar
2 T. salt
2-1/2 c. whole-wheat flour
8-1/2 c. all-purpose flour, divided

Sprinkle yeast into warm water; set aside. In a large bowl, combine milk, oil, sugar and salt; add wheat flour and 2-1/2 cups all-purpose flour. Mix in yeast mixture; add remaining flour. Let rest for 10 minutes; knead for 5 minutes. Allow dough to double in bulk; punch down and allow to double in bulk again. Divide dough into quarters; place into 4 greased 9"x5" loaf pans and let bread double once more. Bake loaves at 400 degrees for 5 minutes; reduce heat to 350 degrees and bake for 30 minutes or until golden.

Nutrition Per Serving: *269 calories, 6g total fat, 1g sat fat, 3mg cholesterol, 611mg sodium, 47g carbohydrate, 1g fiber, 7g protein*

Sweet Avocado Muffins

Farmhouse Bread

Carroty Bran Muffins

Carroty Bran Muffins

Makes 16 large muffins. Serves 16.

2-1/2 c. all-purpose flour
2-1/2 c. bran cereal
1-1/2 c. sugar
2-1/2 t. baking soda
1 t. salt
2 c. buttermilk
1/3 c. applesauce
2 eggs, beaten
1-1/2 c. carrots, peeled and shredded
1 green apple, cored and chopped
1 c. sweetened dried cranberries
1/2 c. chopped walnuts
1/4 c. ground flax seed

Mix all ingredients together in a large bowl. Cover and refrigerate batter for up to 2 days, or bake right away. Fill 16 large, greased muffin cups 2/3 full. Bake at 375 degrees for 15 to 18 minutes; do not overbake. Muffins will become moister if allowed to stand for awhile.

Nutrition Per Serving: 261 calories, 4g total fat, 1g sat fat, 19mg cholesterol, 399mg sodium, 54g carbohydrate, 6g fiber, 6g protein

Quick tip

Need a quick gift for a new neighbor? Line a basket with a pretty cloth napkin and fill with healthy muffins. What a treat!

Nutmeg Crunch Coffee Cake

Makes 12 servings.

2 c. all-purpose flour
1 t. baking powder
1 t. baking soda
1/2 t. salt
1/2 t. cinnamon
2/3 c. butter, softened
1 c. sugar
1/2 c. brown sugar, packed
2 eggs, beaten
1 c. buttermilk

In a bowl, mix flour, baking powder, baking soda, salt and cinnamon; set aside. In a large bowl, beat butter and sugars until light and fluffy, about 2 to 3 minutes. Add eggs, one at a time; mix until well blended. Add flour mixture to butter mixture alternately with buttermilk, beginning and ending with flour mixture. Stir well. Pour batter into a 13"x9" baking pan sprayed with non-stick vegetable spray. Sprinkle Brown Sugar Topping over batter. Bake at 350 degrees for about 30 minutes.

Brown Sugar Topping:

1/2 c. brown sugar, packed
1/2 t. cinnamon
1/4 to 1/2 t. nutmeg

Mix all ingredients in a small bowl.

Nutrition Per Serving: 292 calories, 10g total fat, 7g sat fat, 51mg cholesterol, 336mg sodium, 48g carbohydrate, 0g fiber, 3g protein

Fresh-Baked Breads & Muffins

Miss Karen's Coffee Cake
Serves 15.

2-1/4 c. all-purpose flour
3/4 c. brown sugar, packed
3/4 c. butter, diced
8-oz. container plain low-fat Greek yogurt
1 egg, beaten
1 t. vanilla extract
1/4 t. ground ginger
1 t. baking soda
3 T. sugar
1 t. cinnamon
1 c. chopped pecans

Mix together flour and brown sugar in a large bowl; cut in butter until crumbly. Press 2-3/4 cups of mixture into a greased 13"x9" baking pan; set aside remaining mixture. In a separate bowl, combine yogurt, egg, vanilla, ginger and baking soda; add remaining crumbly mixture. Pour over crust. In a small bowl, combine sugar, cinnamon and pecans; sprinkle over yogurt mixture. Bake at 350 degrees for 25 to 30 minutes.

Nutrition Per Serving: *246 calories, 13g total fat, 6g sat fat, 35mg cholesterol, 145mg sodium, 27g carbohydrate, 0g fiber, 4g protein*

Miss Karen's Coffee Cake

Pretzel Twists
Serves 24.

2 16-oz. loaves frozen bread dough, thawed
1 egg white, beaten
1 t. water
coarse salt to taste

Divide dough into twenty-four, 1-1/2 inch balls. Roll each ball into a rope 14 inches long. Shape as desired; arrange one inch apart on lightly greased baking sheets. Let rise in a warm place for 20 minutes. Whisk together egg white and water; brush over pretzels. Sprinkle with salt. Place a shallow pan with one inch of boiling water on bottom rack of oven. Bake pretzels on rack above water at 350 degrees for 20 minutes, or until golden.

Nutrition Per Serving: *102 calories, 1g total fat, 0g sat fat, 0mg cholesterol, 361mg sodium, 18g carbohydrate, 1g fiber, 3g protein*

Raspberry Yogurt Muffins
Serves 12.

1 c. quick-cooking oats, uncooked
1/2 c. brown sugar, packed
1 c. plain yogurt
1/2 c. canola oil
1 egg, beaten
1 c. all-purpose flour
1 t. baking powder
1/2 t. baking soda
1 c. raspberries, finely chopped

In a bowl, combine oats, brown sugar, yogurt, oil and egg. Beat well; let stand 5 minutes. Sift in flour, baking power and baking soda. Before stirring, sprinkle fruit over flour mixture. Stir to blend. Fill greased muffin cups 2/3 full. Bake at 400 degrees for 20 minutes.

Nutrition Per Serving: *190 calories, 10g total fat, 2g sat fat, 12mg cholesterol, 104mg sodium, 23g carbohydrate, 1g fiber, 3g protein*

Pretzel Twists

Fresh-Baked Breads & Muffins

No-Rise Whole-Wheat Bread

Serves 8.

1 c. whole-wheat flour
1 c. white whole-wheat flour
1 T. sugar
1 t. baking soda
1/2 t. salt
1 c. buttermilk
1 egg, beaten
1/4 c. molasses
2 T. butter, melted

In a large bowl, mix flours, sugar, baking soda and salt. Add remaining ingredients except butter; stir well until moistened. Add butter; stir well. Turn batter into a well-greased one-quart round casserole dish. Bake at 350 degrees for 50 minutes, or until a toothpick inserted in the center comes out clean. Loaf will crack on top while baking. Set dish on a wire rack to cool for about 10 minutes; turn out loaf and finish cooling on rack.

Nutrition Per Serving: *169 calories, 4g total fat, 2g sat fat, 27mg cholesterol, 341mg sodium, 31g carbohydrate, 3g fiber, 6g protein*

Tina's Crusty Cornbread

Makes 8 servings.

3 T. butter
1 c. plain yellow cornmeal
1/2 c. stone-ground yellow cornmeal
2 t. baking powder
1 t. salt
1/2 t. pepper
8-oz. container plain Greek yogurt
3/4 c. sour milk or buttermilk
2 eggs, beaten
1/2 c. finely shredded low-fat Cheddar cheese

Add butter to an 8"x8" baking pan or a 9" cast-iron skillet. Place in a 425-degree oven 5 to 6 minutes, rotating pan to coat the sides with butter. In a large bowl, combine remaining ingredients; stir until well combined and glossy. Pour batter into pan. Bake at 425 degrees for 25 to 30 minutes, or until top is golden. Cut into squares or wedges; serve warm.

Nutrition Per Serving: *178 calories, 6g total fat, 3g sat fat, 50mg cholesterol, 575mg sodium, 22g carbohydrate, 2g fiber, 9g protein*

Ginger-Carrot Bread

Serves 16.

3 c. all-purpose flour
2 t. cinnamon
1-1/2 t. ground ginger
1/4 t. baking powder
1 t. baking soda
2/3 c. crystallized ginger, finely diced
3 eggs
1 c. canola oil
1-3/4 c. sugar
2 t. vanilla extract
1 c. carrots, peeled and grated
1 c. zucchini, yellow or pattypan squash, grated

In a bowl, sift together flour, spices, baking powder and baking soda. Stir in crystallized ginger; set aside. In a separate large bowl, with an electric mixer on medium speed, beat eggs until light and foamy, about 2 minutes. Add oil, sugar and vanilla; beat until sugar dissolves. Add carrots and squash; mix gently until combined. Add flour mixture to egg mixture; stir gently. Coat two, 8-1/2"x4-1/2" loaf pans with non-stick vegetable spray. Spoon batter into pans. Bake at 325 degrees for about one hour, until firm and a toothpick tests clean. Cool loaves in pans on a wire rack for 15 minutes. Remove from pans; cool completely on rack.

Nutrition Per Serving: *329 calories, 15g total fat, 1g sat fat, 40mg cholesterol, 83mg sodium, 50g carbohydrate, 1g fiber, 3g protein*

Ginger-Carrot Bread

Lemon-Rosemary Zucchini Bread

Serves 24.

3 c. all-purpose flour
1/2 t. baking powder
2 t. baking soda
2 T. fresh rosemary, minced
2 eggs
1-1/4 c. sugar
1/2 c. butter, melted and slightly cooled
1/4 c. olive oil
1 T. lemon zest
3 c. zucchini, grated

In a bowl, whisk together flour, baking powder, baking soda and rosemary; set aside. In a separate large bowl, beat eggs until frothy; beat in sugar, melted butter and olive oil. Stir in lemon zest and zucchini. Add flour mixture to egg mixture; stir until blended. Divide batter into two 9"x4" loaf pans sprayed with non-stick vegetable spray. Bake at 350 degrees for 45 to 50 minutes. May also spoon batter into 24 paper-lined muffin cups, filling 2/3 full; bake at 350 degrees for 20 minutes.

Nutrition Per Serving: *147 calories, 6g total fat, 3g sat fat, 22g cholesterol, 125mg sodium, 21g carbohydrate, 0g fiber, 2g protein*

Miss Sallie's Light Cornbread

Serves 16.

1/4 c. oil, divided
3 c. self-rising cornmeal
1 c. self-rising flour
1-1/4 c. sugar
2 c. buttermilk
1 c. 2% milk

Divide oil between two 9"x5" loaf pans. Heat pans in a 375-degree oven for about 5 minutes; remove from oven. In a large bowl, mix together cornmeal, flour and sugar; set aside. Combine milks in a small bowl. Tilt pans to coat with oil; pour remaining oil from both pans into milk mixture. Add milk mixture to cornmeal mixture; stir well. Divide batter evenly between pans. Bake at 375 degrees for 55 minutes. Cool before slicing.

Nutrition Per Serving: *207 calories, 5g total fat, 1g sat fat, 3mg cholesterol, 493mg sodium, 40g carbohydrate, 2g fiber, 5g protein*

Mile-High Biscuits

Makes 12 servings.

2 c. all-purpose flour
4 t. baking powder
1/4 t. baking soda
3/4 t. salt
5 T. chilled butter, diced
1 c. buttermilk

Combine flour, baking powder, baking soda and salt in a food processor; add butter. Pulse just until mixture resembles coarse crumbs. Transfer mixture to a large bowl; add buttermilk. Stir until mixture begins to hold together. Turn out onto a lightly floured surface. Working quickly, knead until most of the dough sticks together. Pat out dough into a 12" circle, 1/2" thick. Cut with a biscuit cutter, quickly re-gathering dough until about 12 biscuits are cut. Arrange biscuits in a parchment paper-lined 13"x9" baking pan. Set pan on center oven rack. Bake at 450 degrees for about 10 minutes, until lightly golden. Serve warm.

Nutrition Per Serving: *117 calories, 4g total fat, 3g sat fat, 13mg cholesterol, 416mg sodium, 16g carbohydrate, 0g fiber, 3g protein*

Mile-High Biscuits

Savory Apple-Cheese Bread

Serves 10.

1/2 c. butter, softened
2/3 c. sugar
2 eggs
1 apple, cored, peeled and chopped
1/2 c. shredded low-fat Cheddar cheese
1/3 c. chopped walnuts
2 c. all-purpose flour
1 T. baking powder
1/2 t. baking soda
1/2 t. salt

In a large bowl, combine butter and sugar, beating until light and fluffy. Beat in eggs, one at a time. Stir in apple, cheese and walnuts. In a separate bowl, combine flour, baking powder, baking soda and salt. Gradually stir flour mixture into butter mixture. Pour batter into a greased 9"x5" loaf pan. Bake at 350 degrees for about one hour. Cool for 10 minutes; turn loaf out of pan onto a wire rack.

Nutrition Per Serving: *262 calories, 12g total fat, 6g sat fat, 53mg cholesterol, 458mg sodium, 33g carbohydrate, 1g fiber, 5g protein*

Whole-Wheat Soda Bread

Serves 4.

1 c. all-purpose flour
1 t. baking powder
1 t. baking soda
1/2 t. salt
2 T. sugar
2 c. whole-wheat flour
1-1/2 c. buttermilk
1 T. butter, melted

In a large bowl, combine all-purpose flour, baking powder, baking soda, salt and sugar. Add whole-wheat flour; mix well. Add buttermilk; stir only until moistened. Turn dough onto a floured surface. Knead gently for about 2 minutes, until ingredients are well mixed and dough is smooth. Form dough into a ball; place on a lightly greased baking sheet. Pat into an 8-inch circle. With a floured knife, mark dough into 4 wedges by cutting halfway through the bread to the bottom. Bake at 375 degrees for 40 minutes, or until loaf sounds hollow when tapped. Brush with butter; cool on a wire rack.

Nutrition Per Serving: *363 calories, 4g total fat, 2g sat fat, 11mg cholesterol, 807mg sodium, 75g carbohydrate, 6g fiber, 14g protein*

Cheese & Basil Scones

Serves 12.

2 c. all-purpose flour
1/4 c. shredded Parmesan or Romano cheese
2 t. baking powder
1 t. baking soda
2 T. fresh basil, chopped
1/4 t. pepper
2/3 c. buttermilk
3 T. olive oil
Optional: 1 egg, beaten

In a bowl, combine flour, cheese, baking powder, baking soda, basil and pepper. Add buttermilk and oil; stir just until moistened. Knead gently 3 times on a floured surface. Line baking sheet with parchment paper. On lined baking sheet, pat dough into 12 rectangles. Pull apart slightly. If desired, brush dough with egg to glaze. Bake at 450 degrees for 10 to 12 minutes, until golden. Serve warm or at room temperature.

Nutrition Per Serving: *111 calories, 4g total fat, 1g sat fat, 3mg cholesterol, 214mg sodium, 15g carbohydrate, 0g fiber, 3g protein*

Cheese & Basil Scones

Sweet Apple Butter Muffins

Serves 12.

1-3/4 c. all-purpose flour
1/3 c. plus 2 T. sugar, divided
2 t. baking powder
1/2 t. cinnamon
1/4 t. nutmeg
1/4 t. salt
1 egg, beaten
3/4 c. 2% milk
1/4 c. oil
1 t. vanilla extract
1/3 c. apple butter
1/3 c. chopped pecans

Combine flour, 1/3 cup sugar, baking powder, spices and salt in a large bowl; set aside. In a separate bowl, blend egg, milk, oil and vanilla together; stir into flour mixture. Spoon one tablespoon batter into each of 12 paper-lined muffin cups; top with one teaspoon apple butter. Fill muffin cups 2/3 full using remaining batter; set aside.

Sweet Apple Butter Muffins

Toss pecans with remaining sugar; sprinkle evenly over muffins. Bake at 400 degrees until a toothpick inserted in the center tests clean, about 20 minutes.

Nutrition Per Serving: 203 calories, 12g total fat, 4g sat fat, 27mg cholesterol, 194mg sodium, 21g carbohydrate, 0g fiber, 3g protein

Delicious Dill Bread

Serves 14.

1/3 c. warm water
1 env. active dry yeast
1 c. cottage cheese
1 T. butter, softened
1 T. fresh chives, chopped
2 t. dill weed
2 t. salt
1 T. sugar
1/4 t. baking soda
1 egg, beaten
2 to 2-1/2 c. all-purpose or bread flour
Garnish: additional butter

Heat water until very warm, about 110 to 115 degrees. Add yeast to water and let stand for 5 minutes. Place cottage cheese in a large microwave-safe dish; heat until warmed. Add butter, chives, dill weed and salt to cottage cheese. Add yeast mixture and stir; add sugar, baking soda, egg and enough flour to make a stiff dough. Cover and let rise in a warm place until doubled. Punch down; dough will be sticky. Transfer into two well-greased round casserole dishes or two, 9"x5" loaf pans. Bake at 350 degrees for 45 to 50 minutes. If bread is browning too quickly, cover lightly with aluminum foil. Remove from oven; rub butter over top if desired.

Nutrition Per Serving: 92 calories, 1g total fat, 1g sat fat, 15mg cholesterol, 371mg sodium, 16g carbohydrate, 0g fiber, 4g protein

Delicious Dill Bread

Desserts & Sweet Treats

(tasty smart-calorie goodies)

It is always comforting to know that you can have that little sweet treat without compromising your good health. Stack up just a few calories with Royal Strawberry Shortcake, reach for two of Emily's Gingerbread Cookies, and scoop up a spoonful of Fruity Fresh Sorbet. So go ahead, lighten up a little...there is always room for dessert!

Healthy Oatmeal Apple Crisp
Makes 8 servings.

6 c. tart apples, cored and sliced
1/4 c. frozen apple juice concentrate, thawed
1 t. cinnamon, divided
1/4 c. butter, softened
3/4 c. quick-cooking oats, uncooked
1/4 c. whole-wheat flour
1/3 c. brown sugar, packed

In a bowl, combine apples, apple juice concentrate and 1/2 teaspoon cinnamon. Stir until well mixed. Spread in an 8"x8" glass baking pan sprayed with non-stick vegetable spray. In the same bowl, mix remaining cinnamon and other ingredients until crumbly; sprinkle over apples. Bake, uncovered, at 375 degrees for 25 to 35 minutes, until apples are tender and topping is golden. Serve warm.

Nutrition Per Serving: *177 calories, 6g total fat, 4g sat fat, 15mg cholesterol, 6mg sodium, 30g carbohydrate, 5g fiber, 2g protein*

Emily's Gingerbread Cookies
Makes 40 cookies. Serves 40.

1/3 c. brown sugar, packed
1/3 c. shortening
2/3 c. molasses
1 egg, beaten
3 c. all-purpose flour
1 T. baking powder
1-1/2 t. ground ginger
1/2 t. salt

Blend together brown sugar and shortening until light and fluffy. Beat in molasses. Add egg, beating well. In a separate bowl, sift together flour, baking powder, ginger and salt. Add flour mixture to sugar mixture; mix well. Cover and refrigerate for 2 hours. Divide dough into fourths. On a floured surface, roll out to 1/4-inch thickness. Cut with cookie cutters. Place on greased baking sheets. Bake at 350 degrees for 5 to 7 minutes, until dark golden. Cool slightly on pans before removing to wire racks to cool completely. Decorate with Frosting as desired.

Frosting:
2-1/2 c. powdered sugar
3 T. butter, melted
3 T. milk
1 T. vanilla extract
1 t. lemon juice

Combine all ingredients in a medium bowl. Beat with an electric mixer on low speed until smooth.

Nutrition Per Serving: *111 calories, 3g total fat, 1g sat fat, 8mg cholesterol, 70mg sodium, 21g carbohydrate, 0g fiber, 1g protein*

Emily's Gingerbread Cookies

Apple Blush Pie

Serves 8.

5 apples, peeled, cored and sliced
1/2 c. sugar
15-1/4 oz. can crushed pineapple
1/3 c. red cinnamon candies
2 T. instant tapioca, uncooked
3 T. butter, softened
2 9-inch low-fat pie crusts

In a bowl, combine all ingredients except crusts. Place one crust in a 9" pie plate; top with apple mixture. Cut remaining crust into 1/2-inch strips; form a lattice pattern over filling. Bake at 425 degrees for 10 minutes. Reduce temperature to 350 degrees and bake an additional 30 minutes. Let cool.

Nutrition Per Serving: *433 calories, 19g total fat, 8g sat fat, 11mg cholesterol, 235mg sodium, 67g carbohydrate, 3g fiber, 2g protein*

Apple Blush Pie

Can't Be Beet Cake

Makes 12 servings.

3 eggs, separated
1 c. corn oil
1-1/2 c. sugar
3 T. hot water
2 c. all-purpose flour
2-1/2 t. baking powder
1 t. salt
1 t. cinnamon
1 t. vanilla extract
1 c. chopped pecans
1 c. beets, peeled and grated
1 c. carrots, peeled and grated

In a deep bowl, beat egg whites with an electric mixer on high speed until stiff peaks form; set aside. In a separate large bowl, combine egg yolks and remaining ingredients. Mix well; fold in egg whites. Pour batter into a greased and floured 12"x8" baking pan. Bake at 350 degrees for 35 minutes, or until a toothpick inserted in the center tests done. Cool. Drizzle with Vanilla Icing before slicing.

Vanilla Icing:

1 T. butter, diced
2 c. powdered sugar
2 teaspoons vanilla extract
2 T. hot water
Optional: food coloring

Mix all ingredients in a bowl until consistency of cream.

Nutrition Per Serving: *514 calories, 28g total fat, 3g sat fat, 55mg cholesterol, 327mg sodium, 64g carbohydrate, 2g fiber, 5g protein*

Can't Be Beet Cake

Blue Pan Cranberry Cake

Berry-Topped White Cupcakes

Makes 24 cupcakes.

4 eggs, beaten
2 c. sugar
2 c. all-purpose flour
2 t. baking powder
1/4 t. salt
1 t. vanilla extract
1/2 c. butter
1 c. milk
Garnish: mixed fresh berries, powdered sugar

In a large bowl, beat together eggs and sugar. Add flour, baking powder, salt and vanilla; mix well and set aside. In a saucepan over medium heat, combine butter and milk. Bring to a boil; cool slightly and add to batter. Mix well. Pour batter into paper-lined muffin cups, filling cups 2/3 full. Bake at 350 degrees for 15 to 20 minutes, until cake tests done. Cool. Garnish with fresh berries and dust with powdered sugar.

Nutrition Per Serving: *152 calories, 5g total fat, 3g sat fat, 46mg cholesterol, 82mg sodium, 25g carbohydrate, 0g fiber, 3g protein*

Blue Pan Cranberry Cake

Serves 8.

1 c. fresh cranberries
3/4 c. sugar, divided
1/4 c. chopped walnuts
1 egg
1/2 c. all-purpose flour
6 T. butter, melted
Garnish: whipped cream or ice cream

Spread cranberries in a greased 9" pie plate. Sprinkle cranberries with 1/4 cup sugar and walnuts; set aside. In a bowl, beat together egg and remaining sugar. Add flour and melted butter; beat well and pour over cranberries. Bake at 325 degrees for 40 to 45 minutes, until golden on top. Garnish as desired.

Nutrition Per Serving: *215 calories, 12g total fat, 6g sat fat, 49mg cholesterol, 10mg sodium, 27g carbohydrate, 1g fiber, 2g protein*

Quick tip

Watch for vintage plates at tag sales. They're just the thing for delivering those special cookies or cupcakes to friends & neighbors.

Berry-Topped White Cupcakes

Just Peachy Blueberry Crisp

Serves 8.

3 c. peaches, pitted, peeled and sliced
1/2 c. blueberries
2 t. cinnamon-sugar
1 c. all-purpose flour
1/2 c. brown sugar, packed
1/4 c. butter
3/4 c. long-cooking oats, uncooked

Arrange peaches and blueberries in a buttered 8"x8" baking pan. Sprinkle with cinnamon-sugar; toss gently to coat. Combine flour and brown sugar; cut in butter and oats. Sprinkle mixture evenly over peaches. Bake at 350 degrees for 40 to 45 minutes.

Nutrition Per Serving: 248 calories, 7g total fat, 4g sat fat, 15mg cholesterol, 5mg sodium, 43g carbohydrate, 3g fiber, 5g protein

Freezy Fruit Pops

Makes 2 dozen pops.

2 T. sugar
2 c. boiling water
20-oz. can crushed pineapple
10-oz. pkg. frozen strawberries, thawed
6-oz. can frozen orange juice concentrate, thawed
5 ripe bananas, mashed
24 3-oz. paper cups
24 wooden craft sticks

In a bowl, dissolve sugar in boiling water. Stir in pineapple with juice and remaining ingredients.

In 2 batches, pour mixture into a blender; process until smooth. Ladle into paper cups; set in a pan. Freeze until partially frozen; insert a stick in each cup. Return to freezer until frozen. To serve, peel away cup.

Nutrition Per Serving: 58 calories, 0g total fat, 0g sat fat, 0mg cholesterol, 1mg sodium, 15g carbohydrate, 1g fiber, 1g protein

Pineapple Upside-Down Cupcakes

Makes 12 cupcakes.

20-oz. can pineapple tidbits, drained and
   1/2 c. juice reserved
1/3 c. brown sugar, packed
1/3 c. butter, melted
1 c. all-purpose flour
3/4 c. sugar
1/2 t. baking powder
1/4 c. butter, softened
1 egg, beaten
Garnish: maraschino cherries

Pat pineapple dry with paper towels. In a bowl, combine brown sugar and melted butter; divide mixture evenly into 12 greased muffin cups. Arrange pineapple chunks over brown sugar mixture. In a bowl, combine flour, sugar and baking powder. Mix in softened butter and reserved pineapple juice; beat for 2 minutes. Beat in egg. Spoon batter over pineapple, filling each cup 3/4 full. Bake at 350 degrees for 30 minutes, or until a toothpick tests clean. Cool in pan for 5 minutes. Place a wire rack on top of muffin tin and invert cupcakes onto rack so pineapple is on top. Cool completely and top each with a cherry.

Nutrition Per Serving: 222 calories, 9g total fat, 6g sat fat, 41mg cholesterol, 29mg sodium, 34g carbohydrate, 1g fiber, 2g protein

Pineapple Upside-Down Cupcakes

Apple Crumble

Makes 8 servings.

1/2 c. butter, softened
18-1/2 oz. pkg. yellow cake mix
1/2 c. sweetened flaked coconut
3 c. apples, cored, peeled and thinly sliced
1/2 c. sugar
1 t. cinnamon
1 egg, beaten
1-1/2 t. vanilla extract
1 c. plain Greek yogurt
Garnish: whipped cream

Combine butter and cake mix in a bowl. Use a pastry cutter or 2 knives to blend mixture until it resembles coarse crumbs; stir in coconut. Pat mixture into the bottom of an ungreased 13"x9" baking pan. Bake at 350 degrees for 8 to 10 minutes, until golden. Arrange apple slices in rows over warm crust. Stir together sugar and cinnamon; sprinkle over apple slices. Blend egg and vanilla into yogurt; drizzle over apples. Return to oven and bake for an additional 25 minutes or until apples are tender. Serve warm with dollops of whipped cream.

Nutrition Per Serving: 507 calories, 22g total fat, 10g sat fat, 58mg cholesterol, 468mg sodium, 73g carbohydrate, 2g fiber, 7g protein

Good Neighbor Sugar Cookies

Makes 3 dozen 4-inch cookies. Serves 36.

3 c. all-purpose flour
1 t. cream of tartar
1 t. baking soda
1 t. salt
3/4 c. butter
2 eggs, beaten
1 c. sugar
1 t. vanilla extract

Mix together flour, cream of tartar, baking soda and salt in a bowl. In a separate bowl, whisk together remaining ingredients with a fork. Stir butter mixture into flour mixture. Wrap dough in plastic wrap; refrigerate for 30 minutes. On a floured surface, roll out dough 1/8-inch thick; cut into shapes with cookie cutters, as desired. Arrange on lightly greased baking sheets. Bake at 375 degrees for 5 to 6 minutes, until lightly golden. Cool. Frost as desired.

Simple Powdered Sugar Frosting:

3 c. powdered sugar
2 T. butter, melted
3 T. skim milk

Mix all ingredients together until smooth.

Nutrition Per Serving: 107 calories, 4g total fat, 2g sat fat, 18mg cholesterol, 78mg sodium, 18g carbohydrate, 0g fiber, 1g protein

Good Neighbor Sugar Cookies

Macadamia Chocolate Chip Cookies

Macadamia Chocolate Chip Cookies

Makes 36 cookies. Serves 36.

2-1/2 c. all-purpose flour
1 t. baking soda
1/2 t. salt
3/4 c. sugar
3/4 c. brown sugar, packed
1 c. butter
1-1/2 t. vanilla extract
2 eggs, beaten
2 c. extra-large milk chocolate chips or chunks
3/4 c. macadamia nuts, chopped
Optional: 1/2 c. sweetened flaked coconut

Mix together flour, baking soda and salt; set aside. In a large bowl, combine sugars; beat in butter and vanilla until fluffy. Add eggs, mixing well. Add flour mixture to sugar mixture and beat until well blended. Stir in chocolate chips, macadamia nuts and coconut, if using. Drop by 1/4 cupfuls, 3 inches apart, onto ungreased baking sheets. Bake at 375 degrees for 10 to 15 minutes, until golden. Makes 2 to 3 dozen cookies.

Nutrition Per Serving: 197 calories, 10g total fat, 5g sat fat, 27mg cholesterol, 81mg sodium, 24g carbohydrate, 1g fiber, 2g protein

Strawberry-Rhubarb Pie

Makes 8 servings.

5 c. strawberries, hulled and chopped
2 stalks rhubarb, peeled and diced
1/2 c. brown sugar, packed
1/2 c. sugar
1/4 c. all-purpose flour
2 T. cornstarch
1/2 t. cinnamon
9-inch pie crust
1-1/2 T. butter, diced

Combine strawberries and rhubarb; set aside. Sift together sugars, flour, cornstarch and cinnamon. Stir into strawberry mixture. Place crust in a 9" pie plate; chill for 10 minutes. Spoon strawberry mixture into crust; dot with butter. Sprinkle Crumb Topping over filling. Bake at 400 degrees for 50 to 60 minutes, or until topping is golden. Set pie on a wire rack to cool for 2 hours.

Crumb Topping:

3 T. all-purpose flour
1 T. sugar
1/8 t. salt
1 T. butter, softened

Mix together flour, sugar and salt; cut in butter until crumbly.

Nutrition Per Serving: 343 calories, 12g total fat, 5g sat fat, 9mg cholesterol, 170mg sodium, 59g carbohydrate, 3g fiber, 2g protein

Strawberry-Rhubarb Pie

Country-Style Skillet Apples

Country-Style Skillet Apples

Makes 6 servings.

3 T. butter
3 T. sugar
1/2 t. cinnamon
2 T. cornstarch
1 c. water
4 Golden Delicious apples, peeled, cored and sliced

Melt butter in a skillet over medium heat. Stir in sugar, cinnamon and cornstarch; mix well and stir in water. Add apple slices. Cook over medium heat, stirring occasionally, until tender, about 10 minutes.

Nutrition Per Serving: 135 calories, 6g total fat, 4g sat fat, 15mg cholesterol, 1mg sodium, 22g carbohydrate, 3g fiber, 0g protein

Homemade Carrot Cake

Serves 18.

4 eggs, beaten
3/4 c. canola oil
1/2 c. applesauce
1 c. sugar
1 c. brown sugar, packed
1 T. vanilla extract
2 c. all-purpose flour
2 t. baking powder
2 t. baking soda
1/2 t. salt
1 T. cinnamon
1/2 t. nutmeg
3 c. carrots, peeled and grated
Optional: 1/2 c. chopped pecans
Optional: carrot curls

In a large bowl, beat together eggs, oil, applesauce, sugars and vanilla. Add remaining ingredients except carrots and pecans; mix well. Stir in carrots; fold in pecans. Pour into a greased 13"x9" baking pan. Bake at 350 degrees for 40 to 50 minutes, until a toothpick inserted in center comes out clean. Let cool in pan for 10 minutes; turn out onto a wire rack and cool completely. Frost; add carrot curls, if desired.

Frosting:

1/4 c. butter, softened
8-oz. pkg. reduced-fat cream cheese, softened
2 c. powdered sugar
1 t. vanilla extract

Combine all ingredients in a bowl. Beat until smooth and creamy.

Nutrition Per Serving: 346 calories, 15g total fat, 4g sat fat, 60mg cholesterol, 345mg sodium, 50g carbohydrate, 1g fiber, 4g protein

Homemade Carrot Cake

Favorite Chocolate Chippers

Makes 36 cookies. Serves 36.

1 c. butter, softened
3/4 c. brown sugar, packed
3/4 c. sugar
2 eggs, beaten
1 t. vanilla extract
3.4-oz. pkg. instant vanilla pudding mix
2-1/4 c. all-purpose flour
1 t. baking soda
1/2 t. salt
12-oz. pkg. semi-sweet chocolate chips
1/2 c. chopped pecans

In a large bowl, beat together butter and sugars. Beat in eggs and vanilla. Add dry pudding mix, flour, baking soda and salt; mix just until well blended. Fold in chocolate chips and nuts. Drop by tablespoonfuls onto greased baking sheets. Bake at 350 degrees for 12 to 14 minutes.

Nutrition Per Serving: 169 calories, 8g total fat, 5g sat fat, 21mg cholesterol, 144mg sodium, 23g carbohydrate, 0g fiber, 1g protein

Quick tip

Surprise your chocolate-chip-cookie-lover friends with a treat they'll never forget! Put a scoop of ice cream between two cookies and make an ice-cream sandwich. Yummy!

Chocolate-Orange Zucchini Cake

Serves 12.

1/2 c. plus 2 T. baking cocoa, divided
2-1/2 c. plus 2 T. all-purpose flour, divided
1/2 c. butter
2 c. sugar
3 eggs
2 t. vanilla extract
zest of 1 orange
1/2 c. milk
3 T. canola oil
3 c. zucchini, peeled and shredded
2-1/2 t. baking powder
1-1/2 t. baking soda
1/2 t. salt
1/2 t. cinnamon
Garnish: baking cocoa

Spray a 10-inch Bundt® pan with non-stick vegetable spray. Mix 2 tablespoons cocoa with 2 tablespoons flour. Coat interior of pan with mixture; shake out any extra and set aside pan. In a large bowl, beat butter and sugar with an electric mixer on medium speed. Add eggs, one at a time, beating well after each addition. Stir in vanilla, orange zest and milk. In a separate bowl, combine remaining cocoa and oil; mix thoroughly. Add cocoa mixture to butter mixture; stir well. Fold in zucchini. Add remaining flour and other ingredients. Beat on low speed until well blended. Pour into prepared pan. Bake at 350 degrees for about one hour, until a wooden toothpick tests clean. Cool in pan for 10 minutes; remove from pan to a cake plate. Cool completely. Dust top of cake with baking cocoa.

Nutrition Per Serving: 364 calories, 13g total fat, 6g sat fat, 73mg cholesterol, 379mg sodium, 59g carbohydrate, 3g fiber, 6g protein

Chocolate-Orange
Zucchini Cake

Tasty Cookie Pops

Tasty Cookie Pops

Makes 4-1/2 dozen.

1 c. butter, softened
1 c. sugar
1 c. powdered sugar
2 eggs, beaten
3/4 c. oil
2 t. vanilla extract
4 c. all-purpose flour
1 t. baking soda
1 t. salt
1 t. cream of tartar
Garnish: sprinkles
lollipop sticks

Beat butter until fluffy; add sugars, beating well. Beat in eggs, oil and vanilla. In a separate bowl, combine flour and remaining ingredients except sprinkles. Add flour mixture to butter mixture and mix until well blended. Cover and chill 2 hours. Shape dough into 1-1/2 inch balls. Roll each ball in sprinkles, pressing gently, if needed, to coat. Place 2 inches apart on ungreased baking sheets. Insert a stick about one inch into each ball. Bake at 350 degrees for 10 to 11 minutes, until set. Let cool 2 minutes on baking sheets; cool completely on wire racks.

Nutrition Per Serving: 124 calories, 8g total fat, 2g sat fat, 13mg cholesterol, 74mg sodium, 14g carbohydrate, 0g fiber, 1g protein

Double-Berry Nut Bars

Makes 9 servings.

2 eggs
1 c. sugar
1 c. all-purpose flour
1/3 c. butter, melted
1/2 c. blueberries, thawed if frozen
1/2 c. cranberries, thawed if frozen
1/2 c. chopped walnuts or pecans
Optional: powdered sugar

In a bowl, with an electric mixer on medium speed, beat eggs until thick. Gradually beat in sugar until thoroughly blended. Stir in flour and melted butter; blend well. Add berries and nuts, mixing gently just until combined. Spread batter evenly in a greased 8"x8" baking pan. Bake at 350 degrees for 35 to 40 minutes, until golden. Cool; cut into squares. If desired, dust with powdered sugar.

Nutrition Per Serving: 262 calories, 12g total fat, 5g sat fat, 65mg cholesterol, 17mg sodium, 36g carbohydrate, 2g fiber, 4g protein

Double-Berry
Nut Bars

Chocolate-Orange Snowballs

Makes 5 dozen cookies. Serves 30.

9-oz. pkg. vanilla wafers
1-1/4 c. powdered sugar, divided
1/4 c. baking cocoa
1/3 c. light corn syrup
1/3 c. frozen orange juice concentrate, thawed
1-1/2 c. chopped pecans

In a food processor, combine vanilla wafers, one cup powdered sugar, cocoa, corn syrup and orange juice. Process until wafers are finely ground and mixture is well blended. Add pecans and process until nuts are finely chopped. Transfer mixture to a bowl; form into one-inch balls. Roll in remaining powdered sugar. Store in an airtight container.

Nutrition Per Serving: 114 calories, 6g total fat, 0g sat fat, 0mg cholesterol, 36mg sodium, 16g carbohydrate, 1g fiber, 2g protein

Chocolate-Orange Snowballs

Eva's Fruit Cobbler

Makes 8 servings.

4 c. rhubarb, sliced
4 c. strawberries, hulled and halved
1 c. sugar, divided
1/4 c. water
2 T. apple juice
1 T. cornstarch
1 c. all-purpose flour
1 t. baking powder
1/4 t. baking soda
1/4 t. salt
1/4 c. butter
1/2 c. buttermilk
1/2 t. almond extract
Garnish: 2 t. coarse sugar

In a large, oven-safe skillet, combine fruit, 3/4 cup sugar and water; bring to a boil. Reduce heat, cover and simmer for 10 minutes. Combine apple juice and cornstarch in a container with a tight-fitting lid; shake well to blend. Stir into fruit and cook until mixture thickens. Keep warm. Combine remaining dry ingredients, including remaining sugar, in a bowl. Cut in butter with a pastry blender or 2 forks until mixture resembles crumbs. Stir together buttermilk and extract; add to dough. Stir to blend well and drop by tablespoonfuls onto hot fruit. Sprinkle with coarse sugar. Bake at 400 degrees for 20 minutes, or until golden.

Nutrition Per Serving: 184 calories, 7g total fat, 4g sat fat, 16mg cholesterol, 188mg sodium, 29g carbohydrate, 4g fiber, 3g protein

Eva's Fruit Cobbler

The Best Oatmeal Cookies

Makes 4 dozen. Serves 24.

1 c. golden raisins
3 eggs, beaten
1 t. vanilla extract
1 c. butter, softened
1 c. brown sugar, packed
1 c. sugar
2-1/2 c. all-purpose flour
1 t. salt
2 t. baking soda
1 T. cinnamon
2 c. quick-cooking oats, uncooked
1 c. chopped pecans

In a small bowl, combine raisins, eggs and vanilla. Cover with plastic wrap and let stand one hour. In a large bowl, combine butter and sugars. In a separate bowl, whisk together flour, salt, baking soda and cinnamon. Add flour mixture to butter mixture; mix until well blended. Stir in raisin mixture, oats and pecans. Dough will be stiff. Drop by rounded teaspoonfuls onto ungreased baking sheets. Bake at 350 degrees for 10 to 12 minutes.

Nutrition Per Serving: 117 calories, 11g total fat, 5g sat fat, 23mg cholesterol, 107mg sodium, 14g carbohydrate, 1g fiber, 2g protein

The Best Oatmeal Cookies

Whole-Wheat Banana Cake

Makes 10 servings.

1-2/3 c. whole-wheat flour
1 c. brown sugar, packed
1 t. baking soda
1 c. ripe banana, mashed
1/3 c. canola oil
1 c. buttermilk
1/2 t. vanilla extract
3/4 c. chopped pecans
Optional: favorite frosting, dried bananas

In a large bowl, combine flour, brown sugar and baking soda; mix and set aside. In a separate bowl, blend banana, oil, buttermilk, vanilla and nuts. Add banana mixture to flour mixture; stir just until moistened. Spoon batter into a greased 9"x9" baking pan. Bake at 350 degrees for 20 to 25 minutes, until center tests done with a toothpick. Cut into squares. Serve warm or cooled. Frost and add dried bananas as garnish if desired.

Nutrition Per Serving: 307 calories, 14g total fat, 1g sat fat, 2mg cholesterol, 152mg sodium, 44g carbohydrate, 4g fiber, 5g protein

Whole-Wheat Banana Cake

Desserts & Sweet Treats

Buttermilk Molasses Cookies

Makes 3 dozen. Serves 36.

1-1/2 c. sugar, divided
1 c. butter
1 c. light molasses
1 c. buttermilk
1 t. vanilla extract
5 c. all-purpose flour
4 t. baking soda
1/2 t. salt
1/2 t. ground ginger
1/2 t. cinnamon
Optional: 1 c. raisins

In a bowl, beat together one cup sugar, butter, molasses, buttermilk and vanilla. In another bowl, combine flour, baking soda, salt and spices. Stir flour mixture into sugar mixture; mix in raisins, if desired. Drop by rounded teaspoonfuls 2 inches apart on greased baking sheets. Sprinkle with remaining sugar to cover. Bake at 350 degrees for 12 to 15 minutes.

Nutrition Per Serving: *129 calories, 5g total fat, 3g sat fat, 15mg cholesterol, 184mg sodium, 29g carbohydrate, 0g fiber, 2g protein*

Buttermilk Molasses Cookies

Spiced Apple Crisp

Makes 6 servings.

4 Golden Delicious apples, peeled, cored and sliced
1 c. fresh cranberries
1/2 c. light brown sugar, packed
1/2 c. all-purpose flour
1/2 c. rolled oats, uncooked
3/4 t. cinnamon
3/4 t. nutmeg
1/4 c. butter, softened
Garnish: vanilla frozen yogurt

Combine prepared apples and cranberries in a buttered 8"x8" baking pan; set aside. In a bowl, combine remaining ingredients except garnish. Mix well and sprinkle over fruit. Bake at 375 degrees for 30 minutes, or until top is golden. Serve warm; garnish with vanilla frozen yogurt.

Nutrition Per Serving: *233 calories, 8g total fat, 5g sat fat, 20mg cholesterol, 67mg sodium, 40g carbohydrate, 4g fiber, 2g protein*

Fruity Fresh Sorbet

Makes 4 servings.

1 peach, peeled, pitted and cubed
1 c. mango, peeled, pitted and cubed
1 ripe banana, peeled and mashed
4 T. water
1 T. lemon juice

Place fruit on a wax paper-lined baking sheet. Cover and freeze for about 2 hours, until completely frozen. Combine fruit, water and lemon juice in a food processor; process until smooth. Serve immediately, or spoon into a covered container and freeze up to 2 weeks.

Nutrition Per Serving: *68 calories, 0g total fat, 0g sat fat, 0mg cholesterol, 1mg sodium, 17g carbohydrate, 2g fiber, 1g protein*

Fruity Fresh Sorbet

Warm Apple Cake

Warm Apple Cake

Serves 9.

1 c. all-purpose flour
1 c. sugar
1 t. baking soda
1 t. cinnamon
1/4 t. salt
1 egg, beaten
2 c. apples, peeled, cored and grated
1/2 c. chopped walnuts, divided

Combine first 5 ingredients in a large bowl. Mix together egg, apples and 1/4 cup nuts; add to flour mixture. Spread in a greased 8"x8" baking pan. Bake at 350 degrees for 25 to 30 minutes, until a toothpick tests clean. Serve warm, topped with Caramel Sauce and remaining nuts.

Caramel Sauce:

1/4 c. brown sugar, packed
2 T. all-purpose flour
1 c. water
1 T. butter
1/4 t. vanilla extract

Combine sugar and flour in a saucepan over medium heat; gradually stir in water. Cook and stir to a boil; cook for one to 2 minutes, until thickened. Remove from heat; stir in butter and vanilla.

Nutrition Per Serving: *242 calories, 6g total fat, 1g sat fat, 27mg cholesterol, 212mg sodium, 45g carbohydrate, 2g fiber, 3g protein*

No-Bake Yummy Balls

Makes 2 dozen. Serves 24.

1-1/2 c. sweetened flaked coconut, toasted and divided
1 c. quick-cooking oats, uncooked
1/2 c. creamy peanut butter
1/3 c. honey
1/4 c. ground flax seed
1/4 c. wheat germ
1/4 c. mini semi-sweet chocolate chips
1/4 c. chopped walnuts
2 T. dried cranberries or cherries, chopped
1 t. vanilla extract

Combine 2/3 cup coconut and remaining ingredients in a bowl. Mix well with your hands. If mixture is too dry, a little more honey or peanut butter may be added. Roll into one-inch balls, then roll in remaining coconut. Place in an airtight container; cover and keep chilled.

Nutrition Per Serving: *120 calories, 7g total fat, 3g sat fat, 0mg cholesterol, 42mg sodium, 13g carbohydrate, 2g fiber, 3g protein*

No-Bake Yummy Balls

Peanut Butter Oat Bars

Makes 18 bars. Serves 18.

1/2 c. whole-wheat flour
1 t. cinnamon
1/2 t. baking soda
1/8 t. sea salt
3/4 c. crunchy peanut butter
1/4 c. brown sugar, packed
1/3 c. honey
1 egg
2 egg whites
2 T. canola oil
2 t. vanilla extract
2 c. long-cooking oats, uncooked
1/2 c. sliced almonds
1 c. sweetened dried cranberries or raisins
1/2 c. dark chocolate chips

Whisk together flour, cinnamon, baking soda and salt in a small bowl. In a separate bowl, beat peanut butter, brown sugar and honey with an electric mixer on medium speed. Beat egg and whites in a separate bowl; add to peanut butter mixture. Mix in oil and vanilla. Add flour mixture; stir in remaining ingredients. Spread into a greased 13"x9" baking pan, using the back of a spatula to spread easily. Bake at 350 degrees for 20 to 25 minutes. Cut into squares.

Nutrition Per Serving: *225 calories, 11g total fat, 2g sat fat, 13mg cholesterol, 119mg sodium, 29g carbohydrate, 3g fiber, 6g protein*

Cherry Berry Chocolate Cake

Makes 16 servings.

1/4 c. butter, softened
1/4 c. shortening
2 c. sugar
1 t. vanilla extract
2 eggs, beaten
1-3/4 c. all-purpose flour
3/4 c. baking cocoa
1 t. baking powder
3/4 t. salt
1-3/4 c. milk
3 c. mixed fresh cherries and berries

Blend butter, shortening, sugar and vanilla until fluffy; blend in eggs and set aside. In a separate bowl, combine flour, cocoa, baking powder and salt; add flour mixture alternately with milk to sugar mixture. Stir well. Pour into 2 greased and floured 8" round cake pans. Bake at 350 degrees for 30 to 35 minutes, until a toothpick tests done. Cool and frost cake between layers and on top, putting fresh berries in middle and on top.

Frosting:

4 T. butter, softened
1/3 c. baking cocoa
2 c. powdered sugar
1/4 c. milk
1 t. vanilla extract

To butter, add cocoa and powdered sugar alternately with milk. Mix in vanilla; stir until creamy.

Nutrition Per Serving: *332 calories, 11g total fat, 5g sat fat, 43mg cholesterol, 175mg sodium, 53g carbohydrate, 3g fiber, 5g protein*

Cherry Berry Chocolate Cake

Pumpkin Bars

Pumpkin Bars

Makes 36 bars. Serves 36.

4 eggs, beaten
3/4 c. oil
1-1/2 c. sugar
15-oz. can pumpkin
2 c. all-purpose flour
2 t. baking powder
1 t. baking soda
1/2 t. salt
2 t. cinnamon
1/2 t. ground ginger
1/2 t. nutmeg
1/2 t. ground cloves

Mix together eggs, oil, sugar and pumpkin in a large bowl. Add remaining ingredients and mix well; pour into a greased and floured 18"x 12" jelly-roll pan. Bake at 350 degrees for 30 to 40 minutes, until a toothpick comes out clean. Let cool; frost with Cream Cheese Frosting and cut into bars.

Cream Cheese Frosting:
3 T. light cream cheese, softened
1 T. butter
2 T. milk
1 t. vanilla extract
2 c. powdered sugar

Beat together cream cheese, butter, milk and vanilla; gradually stir in powdered sugar and mix until spreading consistency.

Nutrition Per Serving: *142 calories, 6g total fat, 1g sat fat, 25mg cholesterol, 108mg sodium, 21g carbohydrate, 1g fiber, 2g protein*

Coconut-Lime Macaroons

Makes 3 dozen cookies. Serves 36.

3 egg whites, beaten
3 c. sweetened flaked coconut
1/4 c. sugar
4 T. all-purpose flour
1/4 c. lime juice
1 to 2 T. lime zest
1/4 t. vanilla extract

In a large bowl, combine all ingredients thoroughly. Form into one-inch balls and place 1/2 inch apart on lightly greased baking sheets. Bake at 350 degrees for 12 to 15 minutes, until edges are lightly golden.

Nutrition Per Serving: *48 calories, 3g total fat, 2g sat fat, 0mg cholesterol, 25mg sodium, 6g carbohydrate, 1g fiber, 1g protein*

Coconut-Lime Macaroons

Soft Pumpkin Cookies

Soft Pumpkin Cookies

Makes 30 cookies.

2-1/2 c. all-purpose flour
1 t. baking powder
1 t. baking soda
1-1/2 t. cinnamon
1-1/2 c. sugar
1/2 c. butter, softened
1 c. canned pumpkin
1 egg, beaten
1 t. vanilla extract

Combine flour, baking powder, baking soda and cinnamon in a bowl. Beat together sugar and butter in a separate bowl until blended. Stir pumpkin, egg and vanilla until smooth. Gradually add flour and sugar mixtures and stir well. Drop by rounded tablespoonfuls onto greased baking sheets. Bake at 350 degrees for 15 to 18 minutes, or until edges are firm. Cool on baking sheets for 2 minutes, then transfer to a wire rack. Cool completely; drizzle Glaze over cookies.

Glaze:

2 c. powdered sugar
3 T. milk
1 T. butter, melted
1 t. vanilla extract

Combine ingredients in a small bowl; mix until smooth.

Nutrition Per Serving: *144 calories, 4g total fat, 2g sat fat, 16mg cholesterol, 61mg sodium, 27g carbohydrate, 1g fiber, 1g protein*

Honey Custard Bread Pudding

Makes 10 servings.

6 eggs
1/2 t. salt
4 c. milk
1/3 c. plus 2 T. honey, divided
2 T. butter, melted
1/2 c. raisins
16-oz. loaf Vienna or French bread, torn into one-inch pieces

Beat together eggs and salt; set aside. Bring milk just to a boil in a saucepan over low heat; let cool slightly. Stir 1/3 cup honey and butter into milk. Slowly stir eggs into milk mixture; add raisins. Place bread pieces in a greased 2-1/2 quart casserole dish. Pour egg mixture over bread. Set casserole dish in a larger pan; add hot water to the pan to come halfway up the side of the casserole dish. Bake at 325 degrees for one hour, or until set. About 15 minutes before serving, drizzle remaining honey over top.

Nutrition Per Serving: *295 calories, 6g total fat, 3g sat fat, 135mg cholesterol, 503mg sodium, 48g carbohydrate, 1g fiber, 13g protein*

Honey Custard Bread Pudding

Desserts & Sweet Treats

Wild Blackberry Cobbler

Wild Blackberry Cobbler

Serves 6.

1/3 c. butter, sliced
3 c. fresh blackberries
1/4 c. plus 2 T. water, divided
1-1/4 c. sugar, divided
1/2 t. cinnamon
2 T. cornstarch
1 c. all-purpose flour
1-1/2 t. baking powder
1 c. 2% milk

Add butter to a 9"x9" baking pan. Place in oven at 400 degrees until melted. Meanwhile, in a small saucepan, combine blackberries, 1/4 cup water, 1/4 cup sugar and cinnamon. Simmer over medium heat, stirring gently. Stir together cornstarch and remaining water until pourable; stir into berry mixture and cook until thickened. Remove from heat. In a bowl, mix flour, remaining sugar, baking powder and milk; stir until smooth. Add flour mixture to butter in baking pan; carefully add berry mixture. Bake at 400 degrees for 25 to 30 minutes, until bubbly and crust is golden.

Nutrition Per Serving: 391 calories, 11g total fat, 7g sat fat, 30mg cholesterol, 146mg sodium, 70g carbohydrate, 4g fiber, 5g protein

No-Bake Granola Bars

Makes 16 bars.

1/4 c. coconut oil, divided
1 c. creamy peanut butter
1/2 c. honey
2 c. long-cooking oats, uncooked
2 c. crispy rice cereal
1 c. sweetened flaked coconut
1/2 c. dried cranberries, chopped
1/2 c. mini semi-sweet chocolate chips

Lightly grease a 13"x9" baking pan with a small amount of coconut oil; set aside. In a large saucepan, combine remaining coconut oil, peanut butter and honey. Cook and stir over low heat just until blended and smooth. Remove from heat; add oats, cereal, coconut and cranberries. Stir just until evenly coated and well combined. Let cool about 10 minutes; stir in chocolate chips. Quickly transfer mixture to baking pan; spread evenly with a spatula. Cover with plastic wrap or wax paper; press mixture down evenly and firmly. Refrigerate for one hour before cutting into bars. May be kept tightly covered and refrigerated for up to 10 days.

Nutrition Per Serving: 267 calories, 16g total fat, 7g sat fat, 0mg cholesterol, 132mg sodium, 33g carbohydrate, 3g fiber, 6g protein

No-Bake Granola Bars

No-Sugar Cherry Pie

Serves 8.

5 c. Bing or Rainier cherries, pitted and halved
2 T. lemon juice
2-1/2 t. cornstarch
1/2 t. salt
1 T. butter, diced
1 T. milk
Optional: sugar

Stir together cherries, lemon juice, cornstarch and salt; set aside. Arrange one portion of Homemade Pie Crust dough in a 9" pie plate. Spoon in cherry mixture; dot with butter. Cover with remaining dough. Flute edges and vent top. Bake at 425 degrees for 30 minutes. Brush top with milk; sprinkle with sugar, if desired. Bake for an additional 10 minutes.

Homemade Pie Crust:

1-3/4 c. all-purpose flour
1 t. salt
1/2 c. oil
1/4 c. cold water

Mix together flour and salt. Add oil; mix with a fork. Add water, one tablespoon at a time, mixing gently with a fork after each addition. Divide dough in half, pat into balls and flatten slightly. Roll out one portion of dough on a lightly floured surface. Roll dough to 1/4-inch thickness. Repeat with remaining dough.

Nutrition Per Serving: *300 calories, 16g total fat, 2g sat fat, 4mg cholesterol, 437mg sodium, 37g carbohydrate, 3g fiber, 4g protein*

Gram's Zucchini Cookies

Makes 4 dozen cookies. Serves 48.

3/4 c. butter, softened
1-1/2 c. sugar
1 egg, beaten
1 t. vanilla extract
1-1/2 c. zucchini, grated
2-1/2 c. all-purpose flour
2 t. baking powder
1 t. cinnamon
1/2 t. salt
1 c. chopped walnuts or almonds
6-oz. pkg. semi-sweet chocolate chips

Blend together butter and sugar in a bowl; beat in egg and vanilla. Stir in zucchini. In a separate bowl, combine flour, baking powder, cinnamon and salt; gradually add to butter mixture. Stir in nuts and chocolate chips. Drop by heaping teaspoonfuls onto greased baking sheets. Bake at 350 degrees for 13 to 15 minutes, or until golden. Remove to wire racks to cool.

Nutrition Per Serving: *110 calories, 6g total fat, 3g sat fat, 12mg cholesterol, 47mg sodium, 14g carbohydrate, 1g fiber, 1g protein*

Quick tip

Offer mini portions of rich cake or make smaller cookies so guests can take "just a taste" of something after a big dinner.

Gram's Zucchini Cookies

Peach Melba Pie

Serves 6.

4 peaches, peeled, pitted and sliced
1 c. sugar
5 t. lemon juice
1/4 c. cornstarch
1/3 c. water
3 c. fresh raspberries
9-inch pie crust, baked

In a large saucepan over medium heat, combine peaches, sugar and lemon juice. In a small bowl, stir cornstarch and water until smooth; stir into peach mixture. Bring to a boil; cook and stir one minute, or until thickened. Remove from heat; cool to room temperature. Gently fold in raspberries; spoon into baked pie crust. Chill at least 3 hours to overnight.

Nutrition Per Serving: 326 calories, 16g total fat, 1g sat fat, 0mg cholesterol, 93mg sodium, 62g carbohydrate, 2g fiber, 1g protein

Peach Melba Pie

Fabulous Zucchini Brownies

Makes 18 bars. Serves 18.

1-1/2 c. sugar
1/2 c. oil
2 t. vanilla extract
2 c. all-purpose flour
1/2 c. baking cocoa
1 t. baking soda
1 t. salt
2 c. zucchini, shredded
1/2 c. chopped pecans

Mix sugar, oil and vanilla; set aside. In a separate bowl, whisk together flour, cocoa, baking soda and salt. Blend in sugar mixture, zucchini and nuts. Batter will seem very dry. Pour into a lightly oiled 13"x9" baking pan and bake at 350 degrees for 25 to 30 minutes. Cut into squares.

Nutrition Per Serving: 199 calories, 9g total fat, 1g sat fat, 0mg cholesterol, 200mg sodium, 30g carbohydrate, 2g fiber, 2g protein

Quick tip

Serve brownie sundaes for an extra-special treat. Place brownies on individual dessert plates and top with a scoop of frozen yogurt or low-fat ice cream. Enjoy!

Fabulous Zucchini Brownies

Royal Strawberry
Shortcake

Royal Strawberry Shortcake

Serves 12.

1/4 c. butter
1/2 c. sugar
1 egg, beaten
2 c. all-purpose flour
4 t. baking powder
1/8 t. salt
1 c. milk
2 t. vanilla extract
4 c. strawberries, hulled and sliced
Garnish: light whipped topping, powdered sugar

In a large bowl, blend together butter and sugar. Add egg; mix well. In a separate bowl, combine flour, baking powder and salt. Add flour mixture to butter mixture alternately with milk. Stir in vanilla. Spread batter in a greased 13"x9" baking pan. Bake at 350 degrees for 25 to 30 minutes. Cool; cut shortcake into squares and split. Place bottom layers of shortbread squares on dessert plates. Top with strawberries and one tablespoon whipped topping. Add shortcake tops and more berries and whipped topping.

Nutrition Per Serving: 157 calories, 4g total fat, 3g sat fat, 24mg cholesterol, 72mg sodium, 28g carbohydrate, 1g fiber, 3g protein

Quick tip

Make desserts extra special with a dollop of low-fat whipped topping instead of whipped cream. It tastes so good and is half the calories.

Strawberry-Lime Yogurt Cake

Serves 12.

2-1/2 c. all-purpose flour, divided
1/2 t. baking soda
1/2 t. salt
2 t. lime zest, divided
1 c. butter, softened
1-1/2 c. sugar
3 eggs
3 T. lime juice, divided
1 c. vanilla yogurt
1-1/2 c. strawberries, hulled and diced
1 c. powdered sugar

In a bowl, whisk together 2-1/4 cups flour, baking soda and salt. Mix in one teaspoon lime zest; set aside. In a separate large bowl, blend together butter and sugar until light and fluffy. Beat in eggs, one at a time; stir in one tablespoon lime juice. Add flour mixture and yogurt alternately to butter mixture, stirring just until blended. In a separate bowl, toss together strawberries and remaining flour. Gently mix berries into batter. Pour batter into a greased and floured 10" Bundt® pan. Bake at 325 degrees for 60 minutes, or until a toothpick inserted near center of cake tests clean. Cool cake in the pan for 10 minutes; turn out onto a wire rack and cool completely. Whisk together powdered sugar with remaining lime zest and juice; drizzle over top of cake.

Nutrition Per Serving: 399 calories, 17g total fat, 10g sat fat, 94mg cholesterol, 180mg sodium, 58g carbohydrate, 1g fiber, 5g protein

Chapter

8

Beverages & Smoothies

(delightful drinks to sip)

Toast your healthy lifestyle with a vitamin-packed smoothie, a refreshing lemonade or a warm, comforting cup of coffee. Whip up a rich Strawberry Preserves Smoothie, tuck a cup of warm Maple Hot Chocolate into your hand and stir up a batch of Fabulous Fruit Tea for that next party. You'll find that sampling or sipping that favorite healthy beverage is good for you and as comforting as can be.

Old-Fashioned Ginger Beer

Serves 10.

4 lemons
1 orange
3/4 c. fresh ginger, peeled and coarsely chopped
3/4 c. sugar
3/4 c. honey
2 c. boiling water
1-1/4 c. orange juice
4 c. sparkling mineral water, chilled
crushed ice
Garnish: orange slices

Grate 2 tablespoons of zest from one lemon and one orange. Set zest aside. Refrigerate lemon and orange for slices later. Squeeze 1/3 cup lemon juice from remaining 3 lemons. Set juice aside. Pulse ginger, sugar and honey in a food processor just until combined; spoon into a pitcher. Add orange and lemon zests, lemon juice and boiling water; stir until sugar dissolves. Cool to room temperature. Stir in orange juice. Cover and refrigerate for at least 24 hours and up to 4 days. Strain before serving. Thinly slice refrigerated lemon and orange; add to pitcher. Stir in sparkling water. Serve over ice. Garnish, if desired.

Nutrition Per Serving: 147 calories, 0g total fat, 0g sat fat, 0mg cholesterol, 3mg sodium, 38g carbohydrate, 0g fiber, 0g protein

Banana-Mango Soy Smoothies

Serves 6.

2 c. vanilla or plain soy milk
2 to 3 bananas, sliced and frozen
6 mangoes, pitted, peeled, cubed and frozen
1 T. honey, or to taste

Combine all ingredients in a blender. Blend on high setting until smooth and frothy. Pour into tall glasses.

Nutrition Per Serving: 225 calories, 3g total fat, 0g sat fat, 0mg cholesterol, 42mg sodium, 52g carbohydrate, 5g fiber, 3g protein

Cranberry-Lime Cooler

Makes 8 servings.

6-oz. can frozen limeade concentrate, thawed
4 c. cold water
16-oz. bottle cranberry juice cocktail
1/4 c. sugar-free orange drink mix
ice
Garnish: fresh mint sprigs

Prepare limeade with water in a large pitcher. Stir in cranberry juice and orange drink mix. Pour over ice in tall mugs or glasses. Garnish each with a sprig of mint.

Nutrition Per Serving: 73 calories, 0g total fat, 0g sat fat, 0mg cholesterol, 3mg sodium, 19g carbohydrate, 0g fiber, 0g protein

Cranberry-Lime Cooler

Maple Hot Chocolate

Makes 4 servings.

3 T. sugar
1 T. baking cocoa
1/8 t. salt
1/4 c. hot water
1 T. butter
4 c. milk
1 t. maple flavoring
1 t. vanilla extract
12 marshmallows, divided

Combine sugar, cocoa and salt in a large saucepan. Stir in hot water and butter; bring to a boil over medium heat. Add milk, maple flavoring, vanilla and 8 marshmallows. Heat mixture through, stirring occasionally, until marshmallows are melted. Ladle into 4 mugs; top with remaining marshmallows.

Nutrition Per Serving: 257 calories, 8g total fat, 5g sat fat, 28mg cholesterol, 239mg sodium, 39g carbohydrate, 1g fiber, 8g protein

Fabulous Fruit Tea

Makes 18 servings.

12 c. water, divided
1 c. sugar
9 tea bags
12-oz. can frozen lemonade concentrate, thawed
12-oz. can frozen orange juice concentrate, thawed
3 c. unsweetened pineapple juice
ice

Bring 4 cups water to a boil in a saucepan over high heat. Stir in sugar until dissolved. Remove from heat; add tea bags. Let stand for 8 to 10 minutes to steep; discard tea bags. Pour tea mixture into a large pitcher. Stir in juices and remaining water. Cover and chill; serve over ice.

Nutrition Per Serving: 108 calories, 0g total fat, 0g sat fat, 0mg cholesterol, 1mg sodium, 28g carbohydrate, 0g fiber, 0g protein

Lemon Iced Tea

Makes 10 servings.

10 orange pekoe tea bags
12-oz. can frozen lemonade concentrate, thawed
ice

Place tea bags in a one-gallon pitcher; fill pitcher 3/4 full with cold water. Let steep in fridge for at least one hour; discard tea bags. Add lemonade concentrate; stir well. Chill until serving time. Serve over ice.

Nutrition Per Serving: 66 calories, 0g total fat, 0g sat fat, 0mg cholesterol, 0mg sodium, 18g carbohydrate, 0g fiber, 0g protein

Maple Hot Chocolate

Fabulous Fruit Tea

Beverages & Smoothies

Minty Orange Iced Tea

Makes 8 servings.

6 c. water
8 tea bags
1/4 c. fresh mint, chopped
3 T. sugar
2 c. orange juice
juice of 2 lemons
ice

Bring water to a boil in a saucepan. Remove from heat and add tea bags, mint and sugar; steep for 5 minutes. Discard tea bags; strain out mint. Chill for at least 2 hours. Pour into a large pitcher; add juices. Serve in tall glasses over ice.

Nutrition Per Serving: *44 calories, 0g total fat, 0g sat fat, 0mg cholesterol, 0mg sodium, 11g carbohydrate, 0g fiber, 0g protein*

Raspberry Cream Smoothies

Makes 8 servings.

3 c. frozen raspberries
1 c. banana, cubed and frozen
2 c. orange juice
2 c. vanilla frozen yogurt
2 c. fat-free reduced-sugar raspberry yogurt
2 t. vanilla extract

In a blender, combine frozen fruit and remaining ingredients. Process until smooth; stir, if needed. Pour into chilled glasses.

Nutrition Per Serving: *158 calories, 0g total fat, 0g sat fat, 1mg cholesterol, 56mg sodium, 33g carbohydrate, 1g fiber, 3g protein*

Southern Honey Ice

Makes 12.

2 c. hot water
1/2 c. honey
2 T. lemon juice

Combine all ingredients and pour into an ice cube tray; freeze. Place ice cubes in tall glasses; top with favorite cold beverage.

Nutrition Per Serving: *40 calories, 0g total fat, 0g sat fat, 0mg cholesterol, 0mg sodium, 10g carbohydrate, 0g fiber, 0g protein*

Quick tip

Search out fun napkins and place mats at flea markets, tag sales and discount stores. Just one pretty napkin or placemat under a centerpiece can add color and style.

Raspberry Cream
Smoothies

Beverages & Smoothies

Fresh-Squeezed Lemonade

juice; remove seeds and strain pulp, if desired. In a large pitcher, stir together chilled syrup, juice and remaining water. Chill for several hours to blend flavors. Serve over ice cubes; garnish with lemon slices.

Nutrition Per Serving: 126 calories, 0g total fat, 0g sat fat, 0mg cholesterol, 0mg sodium, 34g carbohydrate, 0g fiber, 0g protein

Go-Go Juice
Makes 12 servings.

16-oz. can frozen orange juice concentrate
10 c. cold water
1/4 c. vanilla-flavored protein powder

Combine frozen orange juice and remaining ingredients in a large pitcher. Whisk or stir until frothy. Keep mixture refrigerated.

Nutrition Per Serving: 28 calories, 0g total fat, 0g sat fat, 5mg cholesterol, 5mg sodium, 5g carbohydrate, 0g fiber, 2g protein

Fresh-Squeezed Lemonade
Makes 10 servings.

1-3/4 c. sugar
8 c. cold water, divided
6 to 8 lemons
ice cubes
Garnish: lemon slices

Combine sugar and one cup water in a small saucepan. Bring to a boil; stir until sugar dissolves. Cool to room temperature; chill. Juice lemons to measure 1-1/2 cups

Nutty Banana Shake
Serves 2.

2 bananas, peeled and frozen
1-1/2 c. 2% milk
2 T. creamy peanut butter
1 T. honey

Slice frozen bananas and place in a blender with remaining ingredients. Blend until smooth and thick.

Nutrition Per Serving: 330 calories, 13g total fat, 4g sat fat, 15mg cholesterol, 169mg sodium, 46g carbohydrate, 4g fiber, 10g protein

Nutty Banana Shake

Mocha Coffee

Makes 10 servings.

6 T. plus 2 t. instant espresso coffee powder
1-1/4 c. fat-free powdered non-dairy creamer
1/2 c. plus 2 t. sugar
3 T. plus 1 t. baking cocoa
1 T. vanilla powder

Combine all ingredients, stirring well. Store in an airtight container. For each serving, add 3/4 cup boiling water to 1/4 cup mix; stir well.

Nutrition Per Serving: *104 calories, 0g total fat, 0g sat fat, 0mg cholesterol, 30mg sodium, 23g carbohydrate, 1g fiber, 0g protein*

Mocha Coffee

Fresh Spinach Smoothies

Makes 4 servings.

1 c. vanilla almond milk
1 to 2 bananas, sliced and frozen
1 c. fresh spinach, torn into pieces, stems removed
1/2 c. ice
Optional: 1 T. honey

Combine milk, bananas, spinach and ice in a blender; process on high setting until smooth. Add honey if a sweeter taste is desired. Pour into glasses to serve.

Nutrition Per Serving: *66 calories, 1g total fat, 0g sat fat, 0mg cholesterol, 51mg sodium, 14g carbohydrate, 2g fiber, 1g protein*

Oh-So-Fruity Lemonade

Makes 2 quarts. Serves 8.

12-oz. can frozen lemonade concentrate, thawed
2 c. cold water
1-1/2 c. mango juice
1/2 c. red or green grapes, halved
1/2 c. pineapple, chopped
1/2 c. mango, peeled, pitted and chopped
1/2 c. strawberries, hulled and chopped
1/2 c. raspberries
ice cubes

Combine lemonade concentrate, water and juice in a large pitcher. Stir in fruit. Serve immediately over ice, or cover and chill up to one hour.

Nutrition Per Serving: *138 calories, 0g total fat, 0g sat fat, 0mg cholesterol, 2mg sodium, 34g carbohydrate, 1g fiber, 1g protein*

Fresh Spinach
Smoothies

Healthy Strawberry Drink

Makes 4 servings.

2 c. fresh or frozen strawberries, hulled
2 c. fat-free milk
1 T. sugar
5 to 7 ice cubes

Combine all ingredients in a blender; process until smooth. Pour into chilled glasses.

Nutrition Per Serving: 75 calories, 0g total fat, 0g sat fat, 3mg cholesterol, 63mg sodium, 14g carbohydrate, 2g fiber, 4g protein

Quick tip

Most beverage recipes make plenty! Sharing those yummy drinks is a good way to connect with old friends or make new ones. Invite a neighbor or co-worker you've wanted to get to know better to come over for a cool drink or a hot cup of coffee. You'll be so glad you did!

Pink Party Lemonade

Makes 8 servings.

6-oz. jar maraschino cherries, drained
12-oz. container frozen pink lemonade concentrate, thawed
1-ltr. bottle sugar-free lemon-lime soda, chilled

Place a cherry in each section of an ice cube tray; fill with water and freeze. Prepare lemonade in a large pitcher, adding water as directed on package. At serving time, stir in soda and serve over prepared ice cubes.

Nutrition Per Serving: 108 calories, 0g total fat, 0g sat fat, 0mg cholesterol, 13mg sodium, 28g carbohydrate, 0g fiber, 0g protein

Just Peachy Coconut Smoothies

Serves 2.

16-oz. pkg. frozen peaches, divided
14-oz. can coconut milk
2 T. unsweetened flaked coconut
1 T. honey
1 t. vanilla extract

Place half the peaches in a blender; reserve remaining peaches for another recipe. Add remaining ingredients to blender; process mixture until smooth and creamy, about 30 seconds. If consistency is too thin, add a few extra frozen peaches to thicken.

Nutrition Per Serving: 503 calories, 45g total fat, 40g sat fat, 0mg cholesterol, 48mg sodium, 17g carbohydrate, 1g fiber, 6g protein

Pink Party Lemonade

Rosemary Lemon-Pineapple Punch

Makes 12 servings.

46-oz. can unsweetened pineapple juice
1-1/2 c. lemon juice
2 c. water
3/4 c. sugar
4 to 5 sprigs fresh rosemary
1-ltr. bottle ginger ale, chilled

In a large saucepan, combine pineapple juice, lemon juice, water, sugar and rosemary sprigs. Bring to a boil over medium heat, stirring until sugar dissolves. Remove from heat; cover and let stand for 15 minutes. Discard rosemary; chill. At serving time, add ginger ale; serve immediately.

Nutrition Per Serving: *342 calories, 0g total fat, 0g sat fat, 0mg cholesterol, 33mg sodium, 83g carbohydrate, 1g fiber, 2g protein*

Rosemary Lemon-Pineapple Punch

Spring Tonic

Makes about 3 quarts. Serves 12.

2 lbs. rhubarb, chopped
4 c. water
3/4 to 1 c. sugar
ice

Combine rhubarb and water in a saucepan; simmer over medium-low heat until rhubarb is soft. Strain and discard rhubarb, reserving liquid. Pour into a large pitcher; add sugar to taste. Chill until ready to serve. Serve in tall glasses over ice.

Nutrition Per Serving: *54 calories, 0g total fat, 0g sat fat, 0mg cholesterol, 0mg sodium, 14g carbohydrate, 0g fiber, 0g protein*

Chai Tea

Serves 20.

1 c. non-fat dry milk powder
1 c. powdered non-dairy creamer
1/2 c. sugar
2 t. ground ginger
1 t. ground cloves
1 t. ground cardamom
brewed black tea

In a large bowl, combine all ingredients except tea. To serve, add 2 tablespoons of mixture to one cup of brewed tea.

Nutrition Per Serving: *54 calories, 1g total fat, 0g sat fat, 0mg cholesterol, 19mg sodium, 9g carbohydrate, 0g fiber, 1g protein*

Chai Tea

Feel-Good Shake

Makes 3 servings.

2 bananas, sliced
2 c. 2% milk
2 c. non-fat vanilla yogurt
1 c. pineapple juice
1 T. honey

Process all ingredients together in a blender until smooth. Pour into tall glasses. Serve immediately.

Nutrition Per Serving: 362 calories, 5g total fat, 2g sat fat, 23mg cholesterol, 192mg sodium, 65g carbohydrate, 2g fiber, 13g protein

Strawberry Preserves Smoothies

Makes 4 servings.

2 T. strawberry preserves
1 c. crushed pineapple
1 c. orange juice
3 c. fresh strawberries, hulled and sliced
8-oz. container low-fat strawberry yogurt
8-oz. container low-fat plain yogurt

Combine all ingredients in a blender; process until smooth. Pour into chilled jelly jars to serve.

Nutrition Per Serving: 220 calories, 3g total fat, 2g sat fat, 9mg cholesterol, 75mg sodium, 39g carbohydrate, 4g fiber, 7g protein

Feel Good Shake

Quick tip

Using canning jars or jelly jars for drink containers is fun and easy. The jars come in a variety of sizes and colors and are inexpensive. Keep a few in your cupboard right along with your other drinking glasses or goblets. Then they will be easy to find and ready to use!

Strawberry Preserves Smoothies

Beverages & Smoothies

Hot Mulled Cider

Makes 20 servings.

1 qt. water
4-inch cinnamon stick
2 t. allspice
1/8 t. ground cloves
1 gal. apple cider
12-oz. can frozen lemonade concentrate
juice of 2 oranges
1/3 c. honey
1 tea bag

Combine water and spices in a large saucepan. Bring to a boil; reduce heat and simmer gently for 20 minutes. Combine remaining ingredients in a large pitcher; mix well and add to saucepan. Simmer until hot; discard cinnamon stick and tea bag.

Nutrition Per Serving: 148 calories, 0g total fat, 0g sat fat, 0mg cholesterol, 20mg sodium, 36g carbohydrate, 0g fiber, 0g protein

Hot Mulled Cider

Spiced Chocolate Coffee

Makes 8 servings.

8 c. brewed coffee
2 T. sugar
1/4 c. chocolate syrup
4 4-inch cinnamon sticks
1-1/2 t. whole cloves

Combine first 3 ingredients in a large stockpot. Wrap spices in a coffee filter and tie with kitchen string; add to pot. Cover and simmer for 20 minutes. Remove and discard spices. Ladle coffee into mugs.

Nutrition Per Serving: 36 calories, 0g total fat, 0g sat fat, 0mg cholesterol, 5mg sodium, 9g carbohydrate, 0g fiber, 0g protein

Blueberry Flaxseed Smoothies

Serves 4.

1 banana, cut into chunks
1/2 c. blueberries
1 c. low-fat vanilla yogurt
1 c. fat-free milk
2 T. ground flaxseed
Garnish: fresh strawberries, blueberries, flaxseed

Combine all ingredients except garnish in a blender; process on high setting until smooth. Pour into glasses. Garnish with fruit and flaxseed.

Nutrition Per Serving: 127 calories, 2g total fat, 1g sat fat, 5mg cholesterol, 73mg sodium, 21g carbohydrate, 2g fiber, 5g protein

Blueberry Flaxseed
Smoothies

Beverages & Smoothies

"Egg" Nog

Makes 10 servings.

1-oz. pkg. instant sugar-free vanilla pudding mix
2 T. sugar
1/2 gal. 2% milk
2 t. vanilla extract
1/2 t. nutmeg

Mix all ingredients well in a large bowl or pitcher; chill.

Nutrition Per Serving: *115 calories, 4g total fat, 2g sat fat, 16mg cholesterol, 232mg sodium, 14g carbohydrate, 0g fiber, 6g protein*

"Egg" Nog

Mom's Fruit Smoothies

Makes 3 servings.

1-1/2 c. fresh or frozen peaches, cut into chunks
2 mangoes, pitted and diced
1 banana, cut into chunks
8-oz. container non-fat plain yogurt
1 T. honey

Combine fruit and yogurt in a blender. Process until smooth; pour into tall glasses.

Nutrition Per Serving: *203 calories, 1g total fat, 0g sat fat, 2mg cholesterol, 59mg sodium, 49g carbohydrate, 3g fiber, 6g protein*

Fruity Yogurt Smoothies

Makes 2 servings

2 6-oz. containers low-fat fruit-flavored yogurt
1/2 c. peach or strawberries, sliced
1 banana, sliced
1 c. orange or pineapple juice
6 ice cubes

Combine all ingredients in a blender; blend until smooth. Pour into glasses and serve immediately.

Nutrition Per Serving: *299 calories, 3g total fat, 2g sat fat, 13mg cholesterol, 111mg sodium, 47g carbohydrate, 2g fiber, 9g protein*

Mom's Fruit Smoothies

Summertime Iced Tea

Makes 10 servings.

4 c. boiling water
2 family-size tea bags
6 leaves fresh mint
6-oz. can frozen lemonade concentrate
1 c. sugar
5 c. cold water
ice cubes
Garnish: fresh mint sprigs

Pour boiling water into a large heatproof pitcher. Add tea bags and mint leaves; let stand for 5 minutes. Discard tea bags and mint leaves. Add frozen lemonade, sugar and cold water, mixing well. Serve over ice; garnish with mint sprigs.

Nutrition Per Serving: 105 calories, 0g total fat, 0g sat fat, 0mg cholesterol, 0mg sodium, 27g carbohydrate, 0g fiber, 0g protein

Island Chiller

Makes 8 servings.

10-oz. pkg. frozen strawberries
15-oz. can crushed pineapple
1-1/2 c. orange juice
1-qt. bottle club soda or sparkling water, chilled
Garnish: strawberries

In a blender, combine frozen strawberries, pineapple with juice and orange juice. Blend until smooth and frothy. Pour mixture into ice cube trays and freeze. To serve, put 3 cubes into each of 8 tall glasses; add 1/2 cup club soda or sparkling water to each glass. Let stand until mixture becomes slushy. Garnish each glass with a strawberry, if desired.

Nutrition Per Serving: 61 calories, 0g total fat, 0g sat fat, 0mg cholesterol, 36mg sodium, 15g carbohydrate, 1g fiber, 1g protein

Quick tip

Making minty ice cubes is easy! Fill an ice cube tray with water and add a sprig of mint to each one and freeze. Pop out a cube and add to your favorite drink. So pretty!

Summertime Iced Tea

Island Chiller

Slow-Cooker Meals

(all-in-one-pot comfort food)

Try not to peek, but lift the lid if you must to get a look at these lightened-up versions of some of your family's favorite dishes! They will all be asking for seconds of Gramma's Smothered Swiss Steak. Slow-Cooker Chicken & Dumplings is a complete meal in one pot! That crowd is no problem to feed when you make Honey-Barbecued Pork in your slow cooker before the big game. So sit back and relax and enjoy the time you save when you let your slow cooker prepare these lightened-up recipes you love so much!

Carol's Sloppy Joes

Carol's Sloppy Joes

Serves 8.

3 lbs. lean ground beef
1 T. fresh chives, chopped
1 T. fresh parsley, chopped
3/4 c. low-sodium beef broth
1/2 c. catsup
1 T. mustard
1/2 c. instant brown rice, uncooked
salt and pepper to taste
8 whole-grain buns, split

Brown ground beef in a skillet with herbs until beef is no longer pink. Transfer to slow cooker and add remaining ingredients except for buns. Mix well. Cover and cook on low setting for 3 to 4 hours. Serve on whole-grain buns.

Nutrition Per Serving: 440 calories, 19g total fat, 7g sat fat, 109mg cholesterol, 478mg sodium, 26g carbohydrate, 3g fiber, 41g protein

Crockery Black Bean Soup

Serves 6.

1 T. olive oil
2 red onions, chopped
1 red pepper, chopped
1 green pepper, chopped
4 cloves garlic, minced
4 t. ground cumin
16-oz. pkg. dried black beans
1 T. canned chopped chipotle chiles
7 c. hot water
2 T. lime juice
1 t. kosher salt
1/4 t. pepper
1 c. plain low-fat yogurt
1/2 c. plum tomatoes, chopped and seeded

Heat oil in a skillet over medium-high heat. Add onions and peppers; sauté until tender. Stir in garlic and cumin; cook one minute. Use a slotted spoon to transfer mixture to a slow cooker. Add beans, chiles and hot water. Cover and cook on high setting for 6 hours. Transfer 2 cups bean mixture to a blender; purée until smooth. Return mixture to slow cooker; stir in remaining ingredients.

Nutrition Per Serving: 328 calories, 4g total fat, 1g sat fat, 2mg cholesterol, 443mg sodium, 55g carbohydrate, 13g fiber, 19g protein

Heartland Barbecued Beef

Serves 8.

2-lb. beef chuck roast, cut crosswise into 1/2-inch slices
1/2 c. onion, chopped
2 cloves garlic, minced
2 c. low-sodium catsup
1/4 c. brown sugar, packed
2 T. low-sodium Worcestershire sauce
1 t. mustard
1/4 t. salt
1/4 t. pepper
8 onion buns, split

Combine all ingredients except buns in a slow cooker; mix well. Cover and cook on low setting for 6 to 8 hours, stirring occasionally, until beef is tender. Serve on buns.

Nutrition Per Serving: 496 calories, 23g total fat, 9g sat fat, 75mg cholesterol, 394mg sodium, 48g carbohydrate, 1g fiber, 28g protein

The Easiest Rice Pudding

Serves 10.

8 c. whole milk
1 c. brown rice, uncooked
1/2 c. sugar
3 eggs
1/4 c. light cream
3/4 c. dried cranberries
2 t. vanilla extract
1/2 t. cinnamon
1/4 t. salt

Spray a slow cooker with non-stick vegetable spray; set aside. In a bowl, combine milk, rice and sugar; mix well. Spoon milk mixture into slow cooker. Cover and cook on low setting for 5 hours, or until rice is tender. When rice is tender, beat together eggs, cream and remaining ingredients. Whisk 1/2 cup of milk mixture from slow cooker into egg mixture. Continue whisking in milk mixture, 1/2 cup at a time, until only half remains in slow cooker. Spoon everything back into slow cooker; stir. Cover and cook on low for one hour.

Nutrition Per Serving: *265 calories, 8g total fat, 4g sat fat, 23mg cholesterol, 140mg sodium, 43g carbohydrate, 1g fiber, 8g protein*

The Easiest
Rice Pudding

Easy Pork & Sauerkraut

Serves 6.

1-1/2 lb. boneless pork roast
32-oz. jar low-sodium sauerkraut
12-oz. bottle beer or non-alcoholic beer
1/2 apple, peeled and cored
1 T. garlic, minced
2 t. dill weed
1 t. dry mustard

Combine all ingredients in a slow cooker; stir well. Cover and cook on high setting for one hour. Reduce to low setting and continue cooking for 5 hours, or until pork is cooked through. Discard apple before serving.

Nutrition Per Serving: *210 calories, 5g total fat, 2g sat fat, 71mg cholesterol, 520mg sodium, 10g carbohydrate, 4g fiber, 26g protein*

Classic Coney Sauce

Serves 16.

3 lbs. extra lean ground beef, browned and drained
28-oz. can tomato purée
1 c. onion, chopped
2 T. chili powder
1-1/2 T. mustard
1-1/2 T. low-sodium Worcestershire sauce
1/2 t. salt
1 t. pepper
1 t. garlic powder

Combine all ingredients in a slow cooker. Cover and cook on high setting for 3 hours, stirring occasionally. Turn heat to low setting to keep warm. Serve over hot dogs.

Nutrition Per Serving: *169 calories, 9g total fat, 3g sat fat, 55mg cholesterol, 352mg sodium, 5g carbohydrate, 0g fiber, 18g protein*

Easy Pork & Sauerkraut

Pumpkin Patch Soup

Serves 6.

2 t. olive oil
1/2 c. raw pumpkin seeds
3 slices thick-cut bacon
1 onion, chopped
1/2 t. salt
1/2 t. chipotle chili powder
1/2 t. pepper
2 29-oz. cans pumpkin
4 c. chicken broth
3/4 c. apple cider
1/2 c. whole milk

Heat oil in a small skillet over medium heat. Add pumpkin seeds to oil; cook and stir until seeds begin to pop, about one minute. Remove seeds to a bowl and set aside. Add bacon to skillet and cook until crisp. Remove bacon to a paper towel; crumble and refrigerate. Add onion to drippings in pan. Sauté until translucent, about 5 minutes. Stir in seasonings. Spoon onion mixture into a slow cooker. Whisk pumpkin, broth and cider into onion mixture. Cover and cook on high setting for 4 hours. Whisk in milk. Top servings with pumpkin seeds and crumbled bacon.

Nutrition Per Serving: *238 calories, 10g total fat, 3g sat fat, 12mg cholesterol, 573mg sodium, 32g carbohydrate, 9g fiber, 8g protein*

Pumpkin Patch Soup

Slow-Cooker Chicken & Dumplings

Serves 8.

1-1/2 lbs. boneless, skinless chicken breasts, cubed and browned in skillet
2 potatoes, cubed
2 c. baby carrots
2 stalks celery, sliced
10-3/4 oz. can low-sodium cream of chicken soup
1 c. water
1 c. 2% milk
1 t. dried thyme
1/4 t. pepper
2 c. reduced-fat biscuit baking mix
2/3 c. whole milk

Place browned chicken, potatoes, carrots and celery in a slow cooker; set aside. In a medium bowl, combine soup, water, milk, thyme and pepper; pour over chicken mixture. Cover and cook on low setting for 7 to 8 hours until chicken is done. Mix together baking mix and milk; drop into slow cooker by large spoonfuls. Cover and cook on high setting for 30 minutes, until dumplings are cooked in center.

Nutrition Per Serving: *306 calories, 5g total fat, 1g sat fat, 55mg cholesterol, 508mg sodium, 40g carbohydrate, 2g fiber, 26g protein*

Slow Cooker Chicken & Dumplings

Slow-Cooker Meals

Slow-Cooked Creamy Potatoes

Serves 6.

4 green onions, chopped
2 cloves garlic, minced
8 potatoes, sliced and divided
1/2 t. salt, divided
1/4 t. pepper, divided
8-oz. pkg. low-fat cream cheese, diced and divided

Combine green onions and garlic in a small bowl; set aside. Layer one-quarter of the potato slices in a greased slow cooker; sprinkle with half of the salt and pepper. Top with one-third each of cream cheese and green onion mixture. Repeat layers twice, ending with potatoes; sprinkle with remaining salt and pepper. Cover and cook on high setting for 3 hours. Stir to blend melted cheese; cover and cook for an additional hour. Stir well and mash slightly before serving.

Nutrition Per Serving: *199 calories, 6g total fat, 3g sat fat, 20mg cholesterol, 352mg sodium, 29g carbohydrate, 2g fiber, 7g protein*

Susan's Slow-Cooker Ribs

Serves 8.

1 T. onion powder
1 t. red pepper flakes
1/2 t. dry mustard
1/2 t. garlic powder
1/2 t. allspice
1/2 t. cinnamon
3 lbs. boneless pork ribs, sliced into serving-size pieces
1 onion, sliced and divided
1/2 c. water
2 c. low-sodium hickory-flavored barbecue sauce

Combine seasonings in a cup; mix well and rub over ribs. Arrange one-third of ribs in a layer in a slow cooker. Place one-third of onion slices over top; repeat layering. Pour water over top. Cover and cook on low setting for 8 to 10 hours. Drain and discard liquid from slow cooker. Pour barbecue sauce over ribs. Cover and cook on low setting for an additional one to 2 hours.

Nutrition Per Serving: *398 calories, 20g total fat, 7g sat fat, 123mg cholesterol, 426mg sodium, 19g carbohydrate, 0g fiber, 32g protein*

Gramma's Smothered Swiss Steak

Serves 6.

1-1/2 lbs. beef round steak, cut into serving-size pieces
1 T. oil
1 small onion, halved and sliced
1 carrot, peeled and shredded
1 c. sliced mushrooms
10-3/4 oz. can low-sodium cream of chicken soup
8-oz. can no-salt tomato sauce

Brown beef in oil in a skillet over medium heat; drain and set aside. Arrange vegetables in a slow cooker; place beef on top. Mix together soup and tomato sauce; pour over beef and vegetables. Cover and cook on low setting for 6 hours, until beef is tender.

Nutrition Per Serving: *381 calories, 20g total fat, 8g sat fat, 111mg cholesterol, 237mg sodium, 10g carbohydrate, 1g fiber, 36g protein*

Quick tip

Tote along a slow-cooker dish to the church supper or neighborhood block party. Plug it in as soon as you arrive. The food will be hot and tasty!

Gramma's Smothered Swiss Steak

Tex-Mex Quinoa Stew

Tex-Mex Quinoa Stew

Makes 8 servings.

1 lb. boneless, skinless chicken breasts
14-1/2 oz. can diced tomatoes, drained
11-oz. can corn
2 cloves garlic, minced
1 c. quinoa, uncooked
1 t. chili powder
1 t. ground cumin
1/4 t. paprika
1/4 t. dried minced onion
1/2 c. fat-free plain Greek yogurt
1 c. reduced-fat shredded Cheddar cheese

Place chicken in a slow cooker. Top with tomatoes, undrained corn, garlic, quinoa and seasonings. Cover and cook on low setting for about 7 hours, until chicken is very tender. Remove chicken to a plate. Using 2 forks, shred chicken and stir back into stew. Serve stew in bowls, topped with a dollop of yogurt and a sprinkle of cheese.

Nutrition Per Serving: 224 calories, 3g total fat, 1g sat fat, 35mg cholesterol, 352mg sodium, 25g carbohydrate, 3g fiber, 24g protein

Slow-Cooker Turkey Breast

Serves 10.

1/4 c. butter, softened
3 T. fresh sage, chopped
3 T. fresh rosemary, chopped
3 T. fresh thyme, chopped
salt and pepper to taste
6-lb. turkey breast, thawed if frozen
1 to 2 onions, chopped
3 cloves garlic, pressed
1/2 c. red or white wine or chicken broth
1/2 c. low-sodium chicken broth

In a bowl, combine butter, herbs, salt and pepper. Rub mixture over turkey breast. Place onions and garlic in a large oval slow cooker. Arrange turkey breast on top. Add wine, if using, and broth. Cover and cook on low setting for 8 to 10 hours, or on high setting for 4 to 5 hours.

Nutrition Per Serving: 368 calories, 6g total fat, 3g sat fat, 180mg cholesterol, 171mg sodium, 2g carbohydrate, 0g fiber, 67g protein

Orange & Ginger Beef Short Ribs

Serves 8.

1/3 c. low-sodium soy sauce
3 T. brown sugar, packed
3 T. white vinegar
2 cloves garlic, minced
1/2 t. chili powder
1 T. fresh ginger, peeled and minced
3 lbs. boneless lean beef short ribs
1/3 c. orange marmalade
4 cups brown rice, cooked

In a large plastic zipping bag, combine all ingredients except ribs, marmalade and rice. Add ribs to bag; turn to coat well. Refrigerate at least 2 hours to overnight. Drain ribs, reserving marinade. Place ribs in a slow cooker. Add marmalade to reserved marinade; mix well and pour over ribs. Cover and cook on low setting for 6 to 8 hours. Serve over brown rice.

Nutrition Per Serving: 455 calories, 18g total fat, 7g sat fat, 99mg cholesterol, 438mg sodium, 36g carbohydrate, 2g fiber, 36g protein

Slow-Cooker
Hashbrown Casserole

Slow-Cooker Hashbrown Casserole

Serves 8.

32-oz. pkg. frozen shredded hashbrowns
1 lb. ground pork sausage, browned and drained
1 onion, diced
1 green pepper, diced
1-1/2 c. shredded Cheddar cheese
1 doz. eggs, beaten
1 c. milk
1/4 t. salt
1 t. pepper

Place 1/3 each of hashbrowns, sausage, onion, green pepper and cheese in a lightly greased slow cooker. Repeat layering 2 more times, ending with cheese. Beat eggs, milk, salt and pepper together in a large bowl; pour over top. Cover and cook on low setting for 6 hours.

Nutrition Per Serving: 494 calories, 31g total fat, 12g sat fat, 387mg cholesterol, 771mg sodium, 24g carbohydrate, 2g fiber, 28g protein

Chicken Tortilla Soup

Serves 6.

3 boneless, skinless chicken breasts
2 15-oz. cans low-sodium black beans
15-oz. can no-salt corn, drained
2 14-1/2 oz. cans no-salt diced tomatoes with green chiles
1 c. salsa
14-1/2 oz. can no-salt tomato sauce
Garnish: shredded Pepper Jack cheese, low-fat Greek yogurt, crushed tortilla chips

Add all ingredients except garnish in order listed to a slow cooker. Cover and cook on low setting for 9 hours. Remove chicken to a plate; shred and return to soup. Top servings with cheese, a dollop of yogurt and crushed chips, if desired.

Nutrition Per Serving: 282 calories, 2g total fat, 1g sat fat, 17mg cholesterol, 322mg sodium, 50g carbohydrate, 14g fiber, 19g protein

Honey Garlic Chicken

Makes 10 servings.

3 lbs. chicken wings
salt and pepper to taste
1 c. honey
1/2 c. low-sodium soy sauce
2 T. catsup
2 T. oil
1 clove garlic, minced

Sprinkle chicken wings with salt and pepper; place in a slow cooker and set aside. In a bowl, combine remaining ingredients and mix well. Pour sauce over wings. Cover and cook on low setting for 6 to 8 hours.

Nutrition Per Serving: 294 calories, 15g total fat, 4g sat fat, 57mg cholesterol, 451mg sodium, 29g carbohydrate, 0g fiber, 15g protein

Chicken Tortilla Soup

Slow-Cooker Meals

7-Veggie Slow-Cooker Stew

Serves 10.

1 butternut squash, peeled, seeded and cubed
2 c. eggplant, peeled and cubed
2 c. zucchini, diced
10-oz. pkg. frozen okra, thawed
8-oz. can tomato sauce
1 c. onion, chopped
1 tomato, chopped
1 carrot, peeled and thinly sliced
1/2 c. vegetable broth
1/3 c. raisins
1 clove garlic, chopped
1/2 t. ground cumin
1/2 t. turmeric
1/4 t. red pepper flakes
1/4 t. cinnamon
1/4 t. paprika

Combine all ingredients in a slow cooker. Cover and cook on low setting for 8 to 10 hours, or until vegetables are tender.

Nutrition Per Serving: 60 calories, 0g total fat, 0g sat fat, 0mg cholesterol, 195mg sodium, 13g carbohydrate, 3g fiber, 2g protein

Sweet & Savory Beef Sandwiches

Serves 8.

12-oz. can beer or non-alcoholic beer
1 c. brown sugar, packed
24-oz. bottle low-sodium catsup
3 to 4-lb. boneless beef roast
8 whole-wheat rolls, split
Optional: banana pepper slices

Stir together beer, sugar and catsup in a slow cooker. Add roast and spoon mixture over top. Cover and cook on low setting for 7 to 8 hours. Remove roast and shred; return to juices in slow cooker. Serve shredded beef on rolls for sandwiches, topped with pepper slices, if desired.

Nutrition Per Serving: 564 calories, 16g total fat, 6g sat fat, 109mg cholesterol, 424mg sodium, 65g carbohydrate, 3g fiber, 39g protein

Mom's Fall-Apart Sunday Roast

Serves 6.

3-lb. boneless beef chuck roast
salt, pepper and garlic powder to taste
1 T. canola oil
4 potatoes, peeled and quartered
1 onion, quartered
4 carrots, peeled and cut into chunks
1 lb. fresh green beans, trimmed and halved
1 c. water

Sprinkle roast with salt, pepper and garlic powder to taste. Heat oil in a skillet; brown roast on all sides. Place potatoes in a slow cooker; place roast on top of potatoes. Add onions, carrots and green beans. Add water and cover. Cook on low setting for 6 to 8 hours.

Nutrition Per Serving: 736 calories, 43g total fat, 17g sat fat, 150mg cholesterol, 185mg sodium, 37g carbohydrate, 6g fiber, 49g protein

Quick tip

Stir in a little quick-cooking tapioca with other ingredients for a roast or stew. Broth will thicken magically as it cooks!

Mom's Fall-Apart
Sunday Roast

Slow-Cooker Meals

Swiss Steak Colorado Style

Serves 6.

1-1/2 lb. beef chuck roast
15-oz. can diced tomatoes
1 c. red wine or beef broth
1 T. onion powder
1/4 t. garlic salt
1 t. pepper
2 carrots, peeled and sliced
1 onion, diced
1/2 c. low-sodium beef broth
Optional: 1 T. cornstarch, 1 T. water

Combine all ingredients except cornstarch and water in a slow cooker. Cover and cook on low setting for 5 to 6 hours. If a thicker consistency is desired, whisk together cornstarch and water in a cup; drizzle into beef mixture. Cook mixture uncovered, until thickened.

Nutrition Per Serving: *424 calories, 24g total fat, 9g sat fat, 113mg cholesterol, 413mg sodium, 7g carbohydrate, 2g fiber, 34g protein*

Swiss Steak Colorado Style

Honey-Barbecued Pork

Makes 8 servings.

3-lb. pork roast
1 onion, chopped
12-oz. bottle low-sodium barbecue sauce
1/4 c. honey
8 sandwich rolls, split

Place pork in a slow cooker. Add onion, barbecue sauce and honey. Cover and cook on low setting for 6 to 8 hours. Shred or chop pork and serve on rolls.

Nutrition Per Serving: *479 calories, 13g total fat, 4g sat fat, 94mg cholesterol, 339mg sodium, 46g carbohydrate, 1g fiber, 41g protein*

No-Peek Stew

Makes 6 servings.

6 carrots, peeled and thickly sliced
3 potatoes, peeled and cubed
1 onion, sliced
3 stalks celery, sliced into pieces
2 lbs. stew beef, cubed
1/4 c. all-purpose flour
1 T. sugar
1/2 t. salt
1/4 t. pepper
14-oz. can no-salt tomato sauce

Arrange vegetables in a slow cooker; top with beef cubes. Blend flour, sugar, salt and pepper; sprinkle over beef. Pour tomato sauce over top; cover and cook on low setting for 8 to 9 hours.

Nutrition Per Serving: *540 calories, 28g total fat, 12g sat fat, 93mg cholesterol, 402mg sodium, 41g carbohydrate, 5g fiber, 30g protein*

Honey-Barbecued Pork

Scalloped Potatoes & Ham

Serves 6.

8 potatoes, peeled and sliced
1 c. cooked ham, diced
1 small onion, diced
1/2 c. low-fat shredded Cheddar cheese
salt and pepper to taste
10-3/4 oz. can low-salt cream of chicken soup

In a slow cooker, layer each ingredient in the order given, spreading soup over top. Do not stir. Cover and cook on low setting for 8 to 10 hours, or on high setting for 5 hours.

Nutrition Per Serving: *316 calories, 3g total fat, 1g sat fat, 18mg cholesterol, 575mg sodium, 58g carbohydrate, 4g fiber, 15g protein*

Scalloped
Potatoes & Ham

Sausage-Stuffed Squash

Makes 4 servings.

12-oz. pkg. smoked turkey sausage, diced
1/3 c. dark brown sugar, packed
1/4 t. dried sage
2 acorn squash, halved and seeded
1 c. water

In a bowl, mix together sausage, brown sugar and sage; toss to mix well. Fill squash halves heaping full with sausage mixture; wrap each stuffed half with aluminum foil. Pour water into a large slow cooker; place wrapped squash halves in slow cooker, stacking if necessary. Cover and cook on low setting for 6 to 8 hours.

Nutrition Per Serving: *349 calories, 10g total fat, 2g sat fat, 90mg cholesterol, 708mg sodium, 41g carbohydrate, 3g fiber, 25g protein*

Slow-Cooked Veggie Beef Soup

Makes 12 servings.

1-1/2 lbs. stew beef, cubed
46-oz. can cocktail vegetable juice
2 c. water
5 cubes low-sodium beef bouillon
1/2 onion, chopped
3 potatoes, peeled and cubed
3 c. cabbage, shredded
16-oz. pkg. frozen mixed vegetables

Place all ingredients in a slow cooker. Cover and cook on low setting for 9 hours, or until all ingredients are tender.

Nutrition Per Serving: *241 calories, 11g total fat, 5g sat fat, 35mg cholesterol, 543mg sodium, 23g carbohydrate, 3g fiber, 13g protein*

Sausage-Stuffed Squash

Hearty Red Beans & Rice

Serves 8.

16-oz. pkg. dried kidney beans
2 T. oil
1 onion, chopped
3 stalks celery, chopped
1 green pepper, chopped
2 cloves garlic, minced
3 c. water
2-2/3 c. low-sodium beef broth
1/2 t. red pepper flakes
1 meaty ham bone or ham hock
4 c. cooked brown rice
Garnish: chopped green onions, crisply cooked bacon

Soak beans overnight in water to cover; drain and set aside. In a large skillet, heat oil over medium-high heat. Add onion, celery, pepper and garlic; sauté until onion is translucent, 5 to 6 minutes. Place in a slow cooker along with drained beans, water, broth and red pepper flakes. Add ham bone and push down into mixture. Cover and cook on low setting until beans are very tender, 9 to 10 hours. Remove ham bone; dice meat and return to slow cooker. Serve beans spooned over hot cooked rice in bowls. Garnish with green onions and bacon.

Nutrition Per Serving: *452 calories, 11g total fat, 2g sat fat, 35mg cholesterol, 521mg sodium, 60g carbohydrate, 11g fiber, 30g protein*

Chunky Applesauce

Makes 8 servings.

10 apples, peeled, cored and cubed
1/2 c. water
1/4 c. sugar
Optional: 1 t. cinnamon

Combine all ingredients in a slow cooker; toss to mix. Cover and cook on low setting for 8 to 10 hours. Serve warm or keep refrigerated in a covered container.

Nutrition Per Serving: *121 calories, 0g total fat, 0g sat fat, 0mg cholesterol, 0mg sodium, 32g carbohydrate, 3g fiber, 1g protein*

Lillian's Beef Stew

Serves 8.

2 lbs. stew beef, cubed
2 potatoes, peeled and quartered
3 stalks, celery, diced
4 carrots, peeled and thickly sliced
2 onions, quartered
1/2 t. dried basil
1/3 c. quick-cooking tapioca, uncooked
1/2 t. salt
1/4 t. pepper
1 T. sugar
2 c. cocktail vegetable juice

Arrange beef and vegetables in a slow cooker. Combine remaining ingredients; pour into slow cooker. Cover and cook on low setting for 8 to 10 hours.

Nutrition Per Serving: *331 calories, 5g total fat, 2g sat fat, 70mg cholesterol, 446mg sodium, 26g carbohydrate, 3g fiber, 26g protein*

Chunky Applesauce

Easy Beef Goulash

Easy Beef Goulash

Serves 6.

1/2 c. all-purpose flour
1 T. paprika
salt and pepper to taste
1-1/2 lbs. beef chuck steak, cut into 1-inch cubes
1 T. olive oil
6-oz. can tomato paste
1/2 t. dried oregano
1/2 t. dried basil
1 small red onion, sliced

Combine flour, paprika, salt and pepper in a small bowl. Dredge beef cubes in mixture; brown beef in hot oil in a skillet. Place beef in a slow cooker; top with tomato paste, herbs and onion. Add just enough water to cover meat; stir to blend. Cover and cook on low setting for 5 to 6 hours.

Nutrition Per Serving: 387 calories, 23g total fat, 8g sat fat, 74mg cholesterol, 163mg sodium, 20g carbohydrate, 3g fiber, 24g protein

Dad's Famous Minestrone

Serves 10.

4 carrots, peeled and sliced
1 c. celery, chopped
1 c. onion, chopped
5 to 6 redskin potatoes, diced
3 zucchini, sliced
14-1/2 oz. can no-salt diced tomatoes
15-oz. can cut green beans
8 cloves garlic, chopped
3 T. olive oil
1-1/2 t. dried basil
1 t. dried rosemary
2 T. dried parsley
1/2 t. sea salt
1/2 t. pepper
3 14-oz. cans low-sodium chicken broth
12-oz. bottle cocktail vegetable juice
1 bunch escarole, chopped
15-oz. can low-sodium garbanzo beans
15-oz. can low-sodium cannellini beans
8-oz. pkg. ditalini pasta, uncooked
Garnish: grated Parmesan cheese

To a slow cooker, add all ingredients in order listed except beans, pasta and garnish. Cover and cook on low setting for 8 hours. After 8 hours, stir in beans and pasta; cook for one more hour. Top servings with cheese.

Nutrition Per Serving: 328 calories, 6g total fat, 1g sat fat, 0mg cholesterol, 460mg sodium, 60g carbohydrate, 11g fiber, 14g protein

Dad's Famous Minestrone

Dijon-Ginger Carrots

Zippy Chile Verde

Serves 8.

3 T. olive oil
1/2 c. onion, chopped
2 cloves garlic, minced
3-lb. boneless pork shoulder, cubed
4 7-oz. cans green salsa
4-oz. can diced jalapeño peppers
14-1/2 oz. can no-salt diced tomatoes

Heat oil in a large skillet over medium heat. Add onion and garlic to oil; cook and stir until fragrant, about 2 minutes. Add pork to skillet; cook until browned on all sides. Transfer pork mixture to a slow cooker; stir in salsa, jalapeño peppers and tomatoes with juice. Cover and cook on high setting for 3 hours. Turn to low setting; cover and cook for 4 to 5 more hours.

Nutrition Per Serving: 332 calories, 16g total fat, 4g sat fat, 111mg cholesterol, 668mg sodium, 10g carbohydrate, 1g fiber, 34g protein

Dijon-Ginger Carrots

Makes 12 servings.

12 carrots, peeled and sliced 1/4-inch thick
1/3 c. Dijon mustard
1/2 c. brown sugar, packed
1 t. fresh ginger, peeled and minced
1/4 t. salt
1/8 t. pepper

Combine all ingredients in a slow cooker; stir. Cover and cook on high setting for 2 to 3 hours, until carrots are tender, stirring twice during cooking.

Nutrition Per Serving: 71 calories, 0g total fat, 0g sat fat, 0mg cholesterol, 261mg sodium, 16g carbohydrate, 2g fiber, 1g protein

Sneaky Good Sausages

Serves 30.

4 4-oz. jars puréed apricot baby food
1/4 c. brown sugar, packed
3 14-oz. pkgs. mini smoked turkey sausages

Stir together baby food and brown sugar in a slow cooker. Cut each sausage into 4 pieces; add to slow cooker and stir again. Cover and cook on low setting for 4 hours.

Nutrition Per Serving: 80 calories, 4g total fat, 1g sat fat, 28mg cholesterol, 386mg sodium, 7g carbohydrate, 0g fiber, 6g protein

Zippy Chile Verde

Index

Index

Index

Index

Index

Soups & Stews

Send us your favorite recipe

and the memory that makes it special for you!*

If we select your recipe for a brand-new Gooseberry Patch cookbook, your name will appear right along with it...and you'll receive a FREE copy of the book!

Submit your recipe on our website at
www.gooseberrypatch.com/sharearecipe

*Please include the number of servings and all other necessary information.

Have a taste for more?

Visit www.gooseberrypatch.com to join our Circle of Friends!

- Free recipes, tips and ideas plus a complete cookbook index
- Get special email offers and our monthly eLetter delivered to your inbox

You'll also love these cookbooks from Gooseberry Patch!

Busy-Day Slow Cooking

Farmers' Market Favorites

Our Favorite Recipes Under 400 Calories

Fresh & Easy Family Meals

Mom Knows Best Cookbook

Our Favorite Recipes for a Crowd

Cook it Quick

Our Favorite Recipes for One or Two

Tastes Like Home

5 Ingredients or Less

150 Best-Ever Cast-Iron Skillet Recipes

101 Breakfast & Brunch Recipes

Slow Cooker to the Rescue

www.gooseberrypatch.com